Curve Patch Quilts
made easy

Trice Boerens

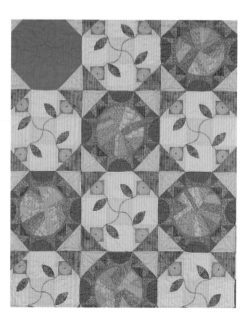

©2005 by Trice Boerens

Published by

kp books
An imprint of F+W Publications, Inc.

700 East State Street • Iola, WI 54990-0001
715-445-2214 • 888-457-2873

Our toll-free number to place an order or obtain a free catalog is (800) 258-0929.

Library of Congress Catalog Number: 2004113671

ISBN: 0-87349-896-8

Edited by Maria L. Turner
Designed by Donna Mummery

Printed in China

Table of Contents

Introduction

It's fortunate, from an aesthetic point of view, that the natural world is defined by organic shapes and curves, rather than straight lines and right angles. We take walks in the woods to experience the rhythm of meandering streams and the grace of bowed branches. To soften our living spaces, we add arched doorways and windows inside, and round-about garden paths outside.

Curved shapes are an important design element to artists because circles, ovals and arcs keep the eye moving within the composition. Curves will also enhance your quilt compositions by breaking up the straight grids that are inherent to most quilt designs. It is easy to stitch two straight edges together, but joining curves can be intimidating because it requires matching and manipulating opposing shapes. Now, you can ease your way into the world of curved seams with the techniques presented in this book. Curves become do-able for three reasons:

- The patterns feature short, loose curves. An even arc is difficult to achieve when the curve is tight, rather than flat.

- The fabric is marked in such a way that seam lines are visible on both layers. It is necessary to readjust the seam lines several times per curve and when stitching lines for the top and the bottom shape are visible, the readjustment can be done quickly and easily.

- The curves are set within a square format. The perimeter of the blocks can be trimmed before assembly. This technique prevents shifting and distortion.

The advantage of trying curved piecing is that adding just a few curves to a block will significantly change its look. The "before" and "after" images of these line art blocks illustrate the differences. The blocks change from being clumsy and rigid to natural and flowing.

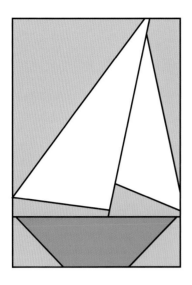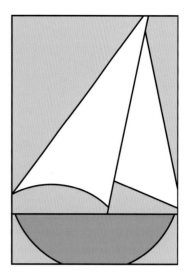

Boat motif "before" (left) and "after."

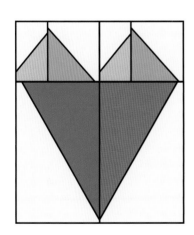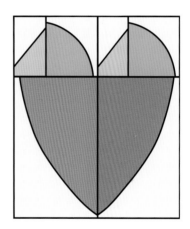

Heart "before" (left) and "after."

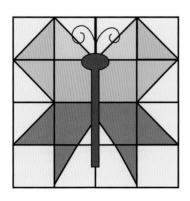

Butterfly motif "before" (left) and "after."

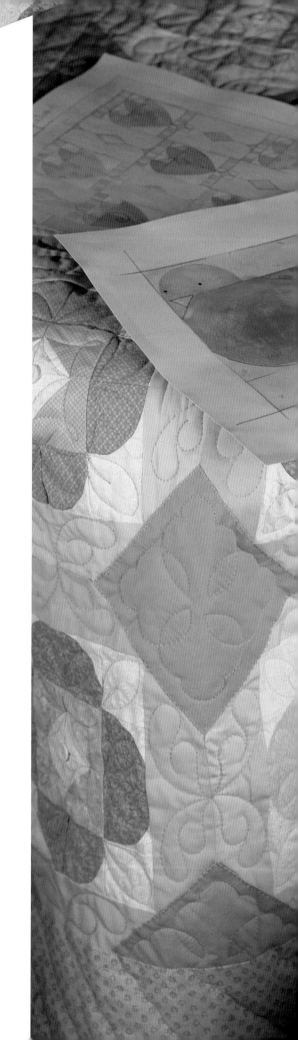

tips and how-to information

General Instructions

The tips and how-to information in this chapter will help you understand the basic techniques that are repeated throughout the projects in this book. Be sure to thoroughly review these concepts before forging ahead.

Selecting Fabrics

Select quality 100% colorfast cotton fabrics. Good fabric should be tightly woven, soft to the touch and free of excess sizing. Since the fabric should be pliant enough to slightly stretch along the concave edge of a curved pattern piece, coated fabrics such as chintz and polished cotton do not work well for the quilts in this book.

Although combining colors and prints is subjective and will reflect personal taste, keep color contrast and print scale in mind.

The fabric requirements within the materials list for each project in this book are based on 44"-wide fabric.

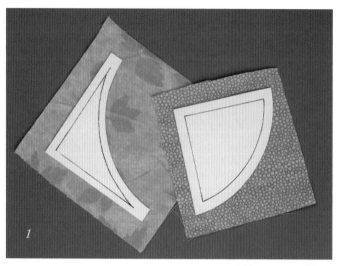

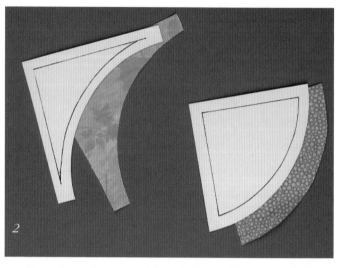

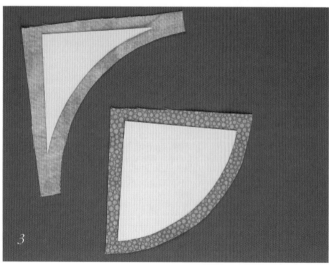

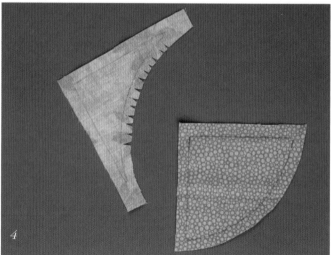

Making Templates

For all of the projects, all seams are ¼". The solid cutting line and the broken seam line are ¼" apart. Use the tracing paper that is listed in each materials list to trace the templates from the book. Since they will be copied multiple times, the templates should be transferred to the cardstock and cut along the solid line.

Here's how:

1 For the concave and the convex curved shapes, transfer both the cutting line and the seam line onto the paper/cardstock, as shown above left.

2 Cut out the shapes, as shown above.

3 Trim the templates to the inner line and then center and place the concave shapes on the wrong side of the fabric and the convex shapes on the right side of the fabric, as shown above left.

4 Use the air-soluble marking pen to mark the seam lines and then cut perpendicular slits in the seam allowance of the concave shape, as shown above. Cut enough slits to make the top shape easy to reposition as you match the top seam line to the bottom seam line.

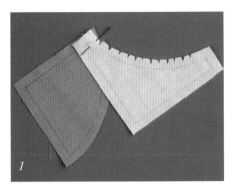

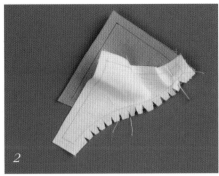

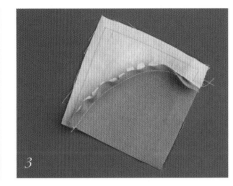

Curved Patch Piecing

Join opposing curves to make a square with a smooth seam line that lies flat when pressed.

The keys to successful piecing are to carefully match the pieces at the dots and to move the top shape without tugging at the fabric.

Here's how:

1 Pin the shapes together at the dot indicated on the templates, as shown

above left. Since the right side of the convex shape and the wrong side of the concave shape are marked, both lines will be visible as you stitch.

2 Stitch the two shapes together, as shown above center, rotating the top shape as you stitch. A more accurate seam will be achieved if you lift the presser

foot, carefully realign the marked lines and reset the presser foot several times per seam.

3 Complete the seam, as shown above, and check the pieced section to make sure there are no distortions and the section is square.

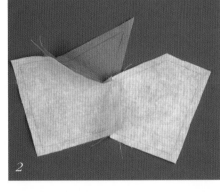

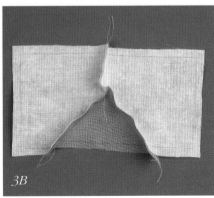

Insetting Diagonal Pieces

For some designs, it is necessary to inset shapes at an angle, rather than joining them with straight seams. Make sure that the stitching lines start and stop at the same point so the block will lie flat when pressed.

Here's how:

1 Stitch the first seam, starting ¼" from the diagonal edge, as shown at left.

2 Matching the raw edges, stitch along the seam line, stopping at the intersection ¼" from the bottom edge, as shown.

3 Realign the raw edges, as shown (3A) and starting at the intersection ¼" from the top edge, stitch the second seam for the completed look shown (3B).

Hand-Appliqué

Also known as "needle-turned appliqué," this technique layers irregular shapes on the quilt with a clean edge. Note: The appliqué templates included in this book have no seam allowances added.

Here's how:

1 On the right side of the fabric, draw around the template with the air-soluble marking pen.

2 Cut around the shape, leaving ¼" seam allowance. Clip the seam allowances at all curves and at inverted corners.

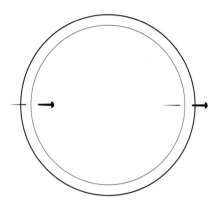

3 Noting the overlaps, pin the pieces in place, as shown above.

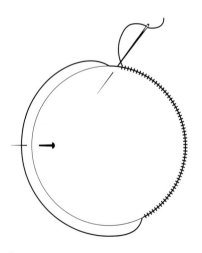

4 Using a fine, sharp needle and short lengths of thread, turn the outside edge under at the marked line and whipstitch the fold to the background fabric, as shown above. Work in short distances of 1" to 2" and crease the fabric with your fingers at the marked line as you stitch.

Hand-Embroidery

Use a sharp embroidery needle and two strands of embroidery floss to add colorful details to the quilt blocks. Cut manageable lengths no longer than 12" and when complete, knot on the wrong side of the fabric and trim the ends.

Wrapped Backstitch

This two-part stitch creates a smooth and even outline.

Here's how:

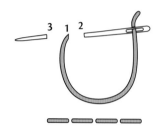

1 The first step is a backstitch worked in reverse (stitch from right to left), as shown above. Use short even stitches and pull the threads with a uniform tension.

2 The second step is a wrapped stitch. Bring the thread up from the back of the fabric and wrap the needle in a spiral sequence around the backstitching, as shown above.

3 After completing the length, insert the needle in the fabric and draw the thread to the back. The needle is inserted through the fabric only at the beginning and at the end of the thread lengths.

French Knot

A French knot is a knot that has the appearance of a small dot.

Here's how:

1 Bring the needle from the back to the front, as shown at right.

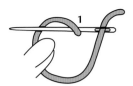

2 Wrap the thread around the needle twice, as shown above.

3 Insert the needle in the fabric next to first insertion point and draw the thread to the back of the fabric, as shown.

Mitered Corner

When the corners of a border are mitered, they are joined at a 45-degree angle. The diagonal seams give the appearance of a picture frame.

Here's how:

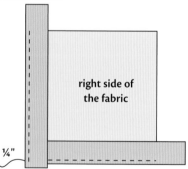

1 Stitch the strips to the sides, starting and stopping ¼" from the corners, as shown above.

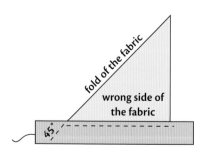

2 Fold the right sides of the adjacent strips together, align the seams and raw edges, and stitch together, using a seam at a 45-degree angle, as shown.

3 After stitching, clip the seam at the intersection and press flat.

Marking the Quilt Top

For a uniform quilting pattern, mark the quilt top with an air-soluble marking pen before layering it with the batting and the backing. Marks from an air-soluble marking pen fade slowly until they disappear. There is no need to remove them.

Water-soluble pens are not recommended because marks from a water-soluble pen require blotting to remove. Often the moistened ink is absorbed by the batting and then reappears on the quilt top.

Quilter's chalk can also be used; however, the lines are fainter and less precise. Quilter's chalk is specially formulated to be removed by light brushing with a cloth or a soft brush.

Freeform quilting patterns or those that follow the seams of the quilt top require no marking.

Pinning and Basting

To secure two or more layers of fabric before stitching, use ordinary dressmaker pins or use basting stitches. Pinning is the quicker alternative, but be careful when stitching over pins. Feed the pins slowly under the presser foot to avoid hitting them with the sewing machine needle, or remove the pins before they move under the presser foot.

Basting stitches are large over-under running stitches done by hand. Since they are temporary, it is not necessary to knot the ends. Use a contrasting thread color to make the basting stitches easy to see and remove.

Machine Quilting

Work from the center out and use both hands to secure the stitching area. Stitch at a slower speed than that of normal machine sewing. As you work, roll the quilt as it accumulates under the arm of the machine.

Binding

A finished binding or "frame" is added to the edge to complete the projects. The narrow strip of fabric should be cut on the bias to allow enough give for an even and flat edge. Be careful to neatly fold the corners for a polished look.

Here's how:

1 Trim the batting and backing even with the quilt top. Leave the first few inches of the binding unattached.

2 Matching the raw edges with right sides together, stitch the binding to the quilt top. At the corners, stop ¼" from the edges.

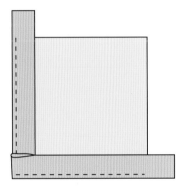

3 Fold the binding at a right-angle, turn the quilt, realign the raw edge of the quilt with the raw edge of the binding and continue stitching, as shown above.

4 When returning to the starting point, fold the edge of the lower binding end under and overlap the opposite end.

5 Fold the binding around the raw edge of the quilt. If you are using prepackaged double-fold binding, handstitch the remaining folded edge of the binding to the back of the quilt. If you are using flat 2½" bias strips, fold the raw edge under and finger-press, as you stitch it to the back of the quilt.

6 At the corners, tuck the binding under to form a diagonal fold.

marking the quilt top

pinning and basting

machine quilting

binding

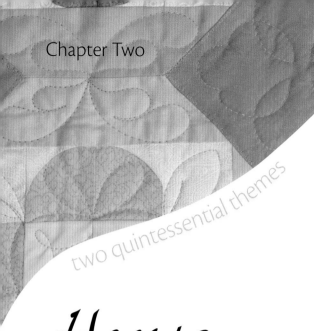

two quintessential themes

Hearts and Flowers

Hearts and flowers: These are two quintessential themes for quilters. Sentimental and decorative, beautiful and garden fresh, these quilts will stitch up easily to brighten up your days.

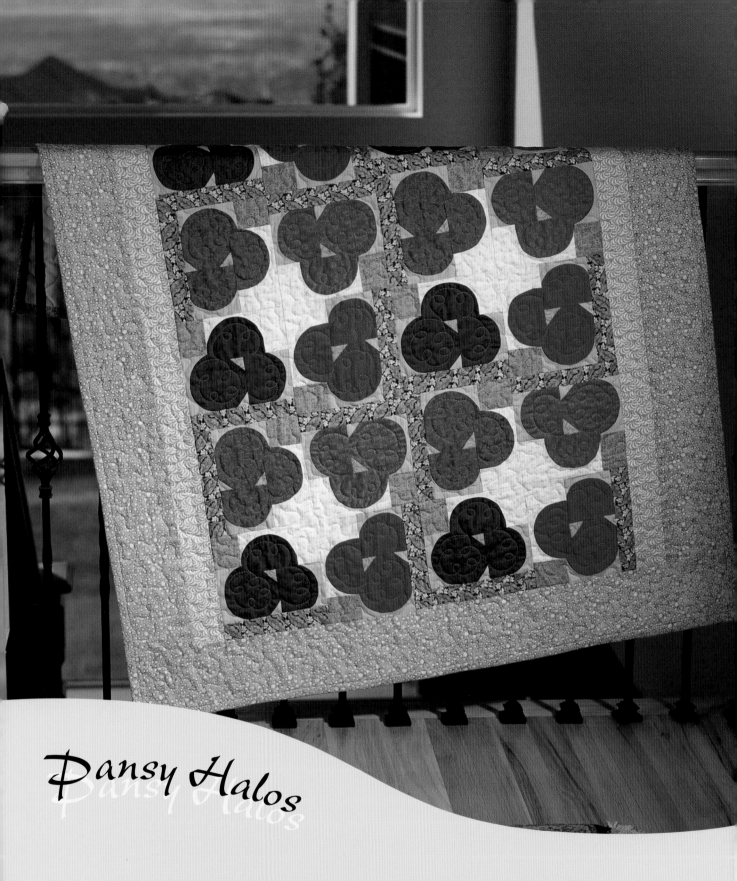

Pansy Halos

This floral arrangement brings to mind border designs of
vintage handkerchiefs. The narrow shape of this quilt makes it
a fitting accent for an entryway or a stairwell.

Materials Needed

- ½-yard periwinkle print (pansies)
- ½-yard lavender print (pansies)
- ½-yard purple print (pansies)
- ½-yard teal print (pansies)
- ⅛-yard gold print (pansies)
- ½-yard ivory print (pansy background)
- ½-yard light green (pansy background)
- ¼-yard green print (pansy background)
- ¼-yard multi-floral print
  (pansy background)
- ¼-yard blue print (border)
- ¾-yard yellow print (border)
- 42" x 52" rectangle cotton fabric (backing)
- 42" x 52" rectangle cotton quilt batting
- 5¼ yards 2½"-wide bias binding or
  prepackaged double-fold bias binding
- Coordinating thread
- 1½ sheets 8½" x 11" tracing paper
- 1½ sheets 8½" x 11" cardstock
- Air-soluble marking pen

Finished size: 40½" x 50½"
The quilt top measures 41" x 51" before quilting. The project
will shrink slightly depending on the amount of quilting.
Seam allowance: ¼"
Templates: Use the templates on pages 18 and 19. Cut on the
solid line and stitch on the broken line.

Cutting Plan

From the periwinkle print, cut:
- six "B" shapes
- six "D" shapes
- six "F" shapes
- six "G" shapes

From the lavender print, cut:
- six "B" shapes
- six "D" shapes
- six "F" shapes
- six "G" shapes

From the purple print, cut:
- six "B" shapes
- six "D" shapes
- six "F" shapes
- six "G" shapes

From the ivory print, cut:
- 24 "A" shapes
- 24 2" x 3¼" rectangles

From the teal print, cut:
- six "B" shapes
- six "D" shapes
- six "F" shapes
- six "G" shapes

From the gold print, cut
- 24 "H" triangles

From the light green, cut:
- 24 "C" shapes
- 24 "E" shapes
- 24 "H" triangles

From the green print, cut:
- 24 2¼" x 2¾" rectangles

From the multi-floral print, cut:
- 24 1½" x 7½" strips

From the blue print, cut:
- two 2½" x 42" strips

From the yellow print, cut:
- four 4¾" x 42" strips

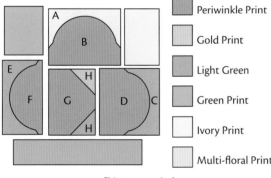

Periwinkle Print
Gold Print
Light Green
Green Print
Ivory Print
Multi-floral Print

Diagram A-1

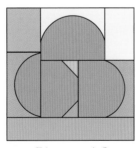

*Diagram A-2:
"A" Pansy Square*

Make the Quilt Blocks

1 Match the curved shapes at the dots
and stitch the specified flower shapes
to the background shapes, as shown in
Diagram A-1. Refer to the instructions
for Curved Patch Piecing on page 9 for
assistance, if necessary. Press.

2 Stitch the sections together to make
an "A" pansy square, as shown in
Diagram A-2. Press.

3 Repeat steps 1 and 2 to make a total
of six "A" pansy squares.

4 Stitch the specified flower shapes
to the background shapes, as in
Diagram B-1. Press.

5 Stitch the sections together to make
a "B" pansy square, as shown in
Diagram B-2. Press.

6 Repeat steps 4 and 5 to make a total
of six "B" pansy blocks.

Lavender Print
Gold Print
Light Green
Green Print
Ivory Print
Multi-floral Print

Diagram B-1

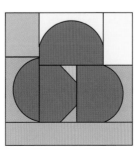

*Diagram B-2:
"B" Pansy Square*

7 Stitch the specified flower shapes to the background shapes, referring to Diagram C-1 and its color code for assistance. Press.

8 Stitch the sections together to make a "C" pansy square, as shown in Diagram C-2. Press.

9 Repeat steps 7 and 8 to make a total of six "C" pansy squares.

10 Stitch the specified flower shapes to the background shapes, referring to Diagram D-1 and its color code for assistance. Press.

11 Stitch the sections together to make a "D" pansy square, as shown in Diagram D-2. Press.

12 Repeat steps 10 and 11 to make a total of six "D" pansy squares.

Assemble the Quilt Top

1 Stitch one of each pansy square together, as shown in Diagram E-1, to make a large square.

2 Repeat step 1 to make a total of six large squares.

3 Stitch the large squares together, referring to the Quilt Layout on the next page for placement. Press.

4 Stitch the blue print strips to the sides of the quilt center, as in the Quilt Layout. Press.

5 Stitch two yellow print strips to the sides of the quilt center, as shown in the Quilt Layout. Press.

6 Stitch the remaining two yellow print strips to the top and the bottom of the quilt center, referring to the Quilt Layout once again. Press.

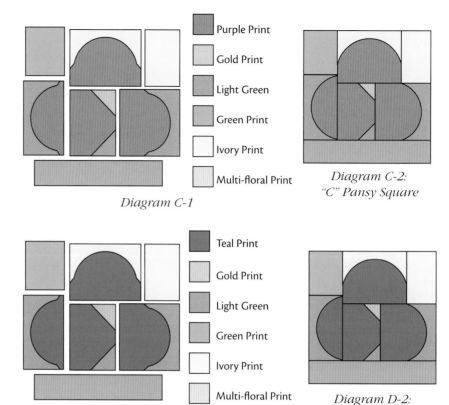

Purple Print

Gold Print

Light Green

Green Print

Ivory Print

Multi-floral Print

Diagram C-1

Diagram C-2:
"C" Pansy Square

Teal Print

Gold Print

Light Green

Green Print

Ivory Print

Multi-floral Print

Diagram D-1

Diagram D-2:
"D" Pansy Square

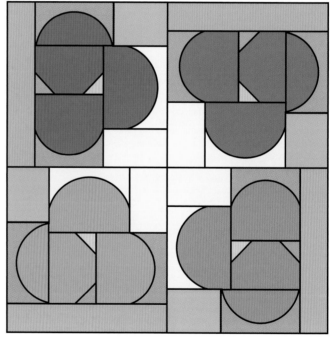

Diagram E-1

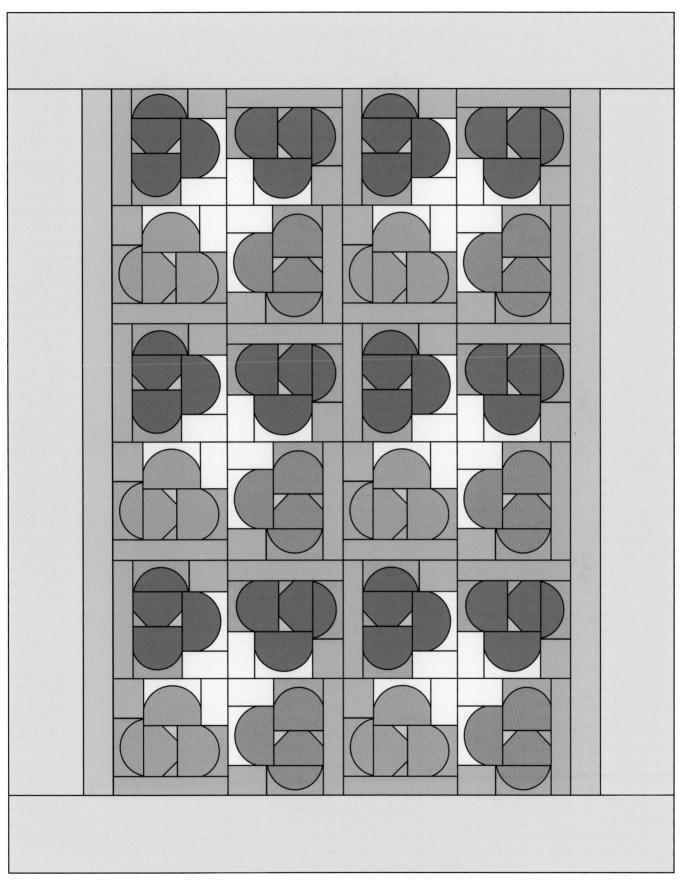

Quilt Layout

Finish the Quilt

1 Review the instructions for Marking the Quilt Top on page 11 and mark the quilting lines on the quilt top with the marking pen.

2 With the wrong side up, place the backing fabric on the work surface. Carefully smooth out any folds and center the batting on the top of the backing fabric.

3 With the right side up, center the quilt top on the batting.

4 Baste through all layers with pins or with long basting stitches, referring back to the Pinning and Basting section on page 11 for assistance, if necessary.

5 Review the Machine Quilting instructions on page 11 and machine quilt as desired.

6 Remove pins or basting stitches.

7 Trim the thread ends and then trim the edge of the quilt.

8 Stitch the bias binding around the edge of the quilt, as detailed in the Binding instructions on page 11.

The back of the quilt shows the detail of the machine quilting used for this particular design.

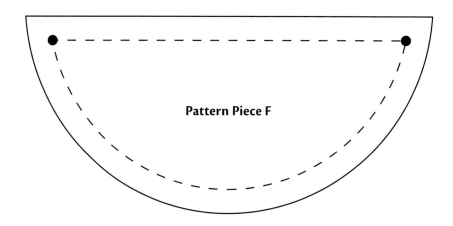

Pattern Piece F

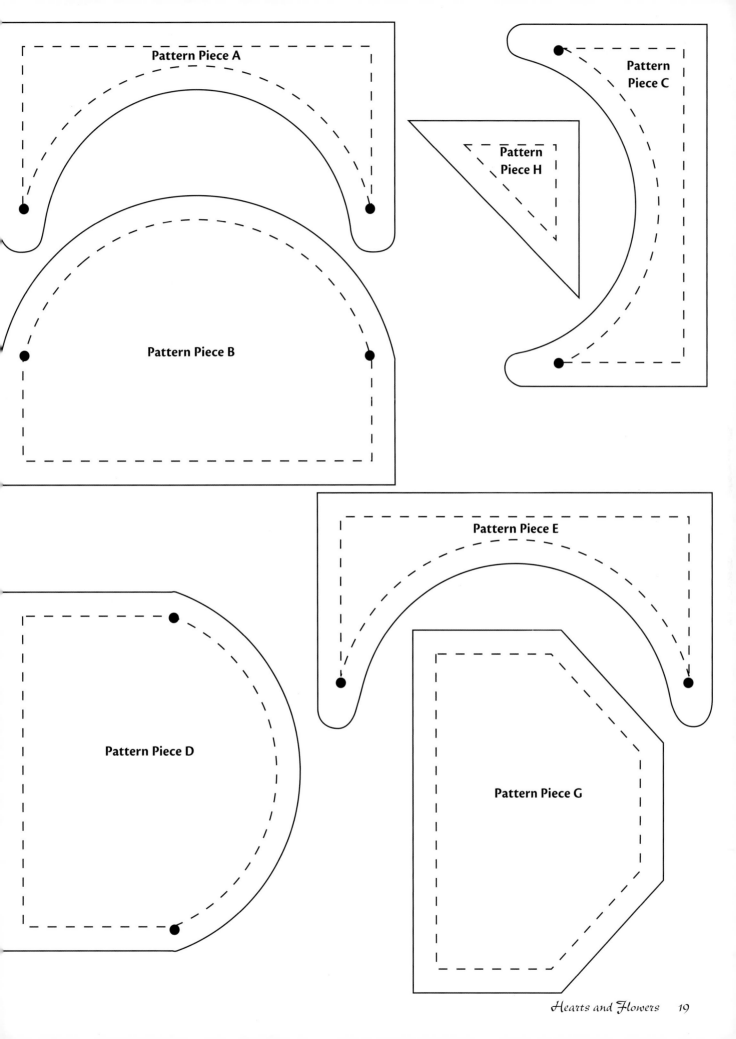

Pattern Piece A

Pattern Piece B

Pattern
Piece C

Pattern
Piece H

Pattern Piece E

Pattern Piece D

Pattern Piece G

Harlequin Hearts

The Harlequins of France were comic entertainers who wore costumes patterned with elongated diamonds. Here, these diamonds are combined with hearts to create a playful and festive quilt.

Materials Needed

- ¼-yard dark pink leaf print (hearts)
- ¼-yard violet print (hearts)
- ⅛-yard pink solid (hearts)
- ⅛-yard pink floral print (hearts)
- ¼-yard blue polka-dot (hearts)
- ¼-yard pink-and-blue multi (hearts)
- ⅛-yard lavender print (hearts)
- ⅛-yard teal mottle (hearts)
- ½-yard peach (heart background)
- ⅛-yard each of 12 to 18 coordinating pastel prints and stripes (heart bands)
- 1 yard cream (solid and diamond blocks)
- ½-yard gold (solid and diamond blocks; also used for border)
- ¼-yard mint print (border)
- ¼-yard lavender print (border)
- ¼-yard tan print (border)
- 46" x 53" rectangle cotton fabric (backing)
- 46" x 53" rectangle cotton quilt batting
- 5½ yards 2½"-wide bias binding or prepackaged double-fold bias binding
- Coordinating thread
- 2 sheets 8½" x 11" tracing paper
- 2 sheets 8½" x 11" cardstock
- Air-soluble marking pen

Finished size: 44½" x 52"

The quilt top measures 45" x 52¾" before quilting. The project will shrink slightly depending on the amount of quilting.

Seam allowances: ¼"

Templates: Use the templates on pages 24 and 25. Cut on the solid line and stitch on the broken line.

Cutting Plan

From the dark pink leaf print, cut:
- nine "A" shapes

From the violet print, cut:
- nine reverse "A" shapes

From the pink, cut:
- 18 "E" shapes

From the pink floral print, cut:
- 18 "C" shapes

From the blue polka-dot, cut:
- nine "A" shapes

From the pink and blue multi, cut:
- nine reverse "A" shapes

From the lavender print, cut:
- 18 "E" shapes

From the teal mottle, cut:
- 18 "C" shapes

From the gold, cut:
- 18 "G" triangles
- nine "H" diamonds

From the cream, cut:
- eight 6" x 9¾" rectangles
- 18 "F" shapes
- 18 reverse "F" shapes

From the peach, cut:
- 18 "B" shapes
- 18 reverse "B" shapes
- 36 "D" shapes
- 36 "E" shapes

From the pastel prints and stripes, cut:
- 18" lengths of between 1" and 2" wide
Cut enough to make six 7" x 18" rectangles.

From the remaining gold, the mint print, the lavender print, and the tan print, cut:
- a total of eight to 10 3½"-wide strips, each strip between 15" and 32" long

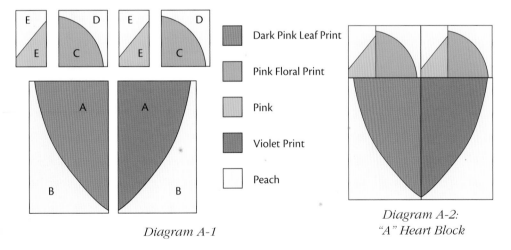

Dark Pink Leaf Print

Pink Floral Print

Pink

Violet Print

Peach

Diagram A-1

Diagram A-2:
"A" Heart Block

Make the Quilt Blocks

1 Match the curved shapes at the dots and stitch the specified heart shapes to the peach background shapes, as shown in Diagram A-1. Refer to the instructions for Curved Patch Piecing on page 9 for assistance, if necessary. Press.

2 Stitch the sections together to make an "A" heart block, as shown in Diagram A-2. Press.

3 Repeat steps 1 and 2 to make a total of nine "A" heart blocks.

4 Stitch the specified heart shapes to the peach background shapes, as in Diagram B-1. Press.

5 Stitch the sections together to make a "B" heart block, as shown in Diagram B-2. Press.

6 Repeat steps 4 and 5 to make a total of nine "B" heart blocks.

7 Stitch 18" lengths of prints and stripes together to make pieced sections of 6" wide or slightly wider. Press.

8 Cut 2"-wide strips perpendicular to the seam line, as shown in Diagram C-1.

9 Repeat step 8 to make a total of 36 strips for the heart block bands.

10 Stitch the bands to the tops and bottoms of the heart blocks. Press.

11 Stitch two "F" shapes together at the tapered sides, as shown in Diagram D-1, starting and stopping ¼" from each edge.

12 Repeat step 11 so that you have one pair.

13 Review the instructions for Insetting Diagonal Pieces on page 9 and stitch the diamonds and the triangles to the "F" shapes, as shown in Diagram E-1.

14 Stitch the "G" triangles in the top and bottom recesses to complete the diamond block, as in Diagram E-2. Press.

15 Repeat steps 13 and 14 to make a total of nine diamond blocks.

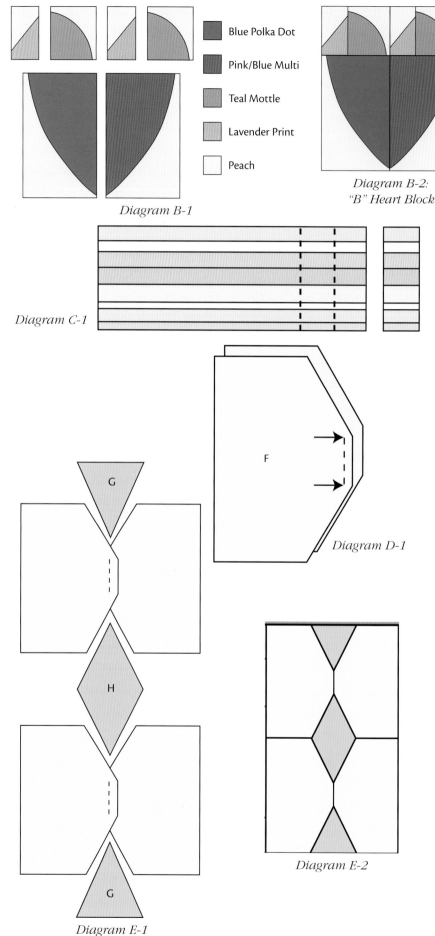

Blue Polka Dot

Pink/Blue Multi

Teal Mottle

Lavender Print

Peach

Diagram B-1

Diagram B-2: "B" Heart Block

Diagram C-1

Diagram D-1

G

H

G

Diagram E-1

Diagram E-2

Assemble the Quilt Top

1 Using heart blocks, diamond blocks and cream rectangles, stitch together the quilt center, as shown in the Quilt Layout below. Press.

2 Stitch the short ends of the border strips together in the desired sequence, referring to the Quilt Layout for assistance. Press.

3 Stitch the pieced strips to the quilt center, as in the Quilt Layout. Press.

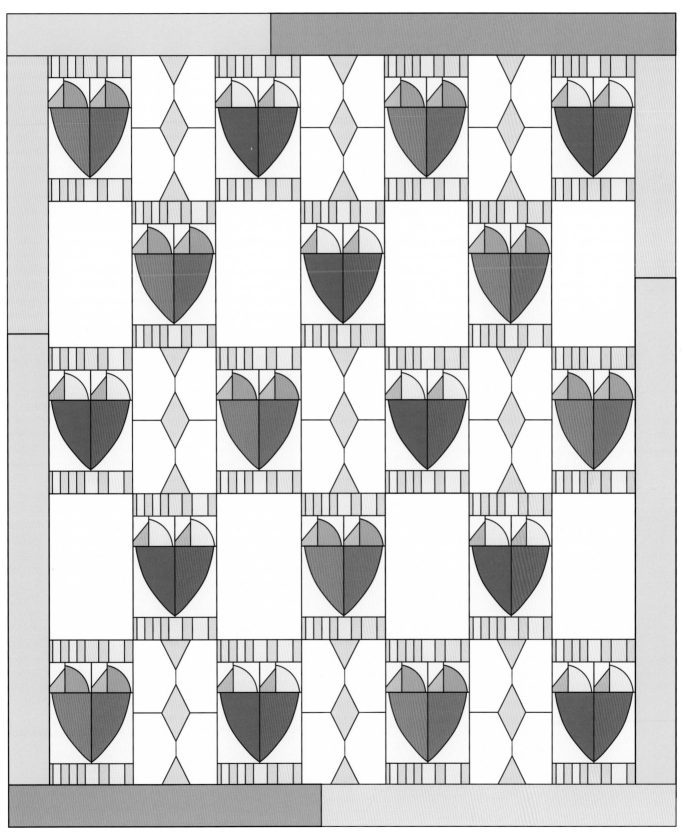

Quilt Layout

The back of the quilt shows the detail of the machine quilting used for this particular design.

Finish the Quilt

1 Review the instructions for Marking the Quilt Top on page 11 and mark the quilting lines on the quilt top with the marking pen.

2 With the wrong side up, place the backing fabric on the work surface. Carefully smooth out any folds and center the batting on the top of the backing fabric.

3 With the right side up, center the quilt top on the batting.

4 Baste through all layers with pins or with long basting stitches, referring back to the Pinning and Basting section on page 11 for assistance, if necessary.

5 Review the Machine Quilting instructions on page 11 and machine quilt as desired.

6 Remove pins or basting stitches.

7 Trim the thread ends and then trim the edge of the quilt.

8 Stitch the bias binding around the edge of the quilt, as detailed in the Binding instructions on page 11.

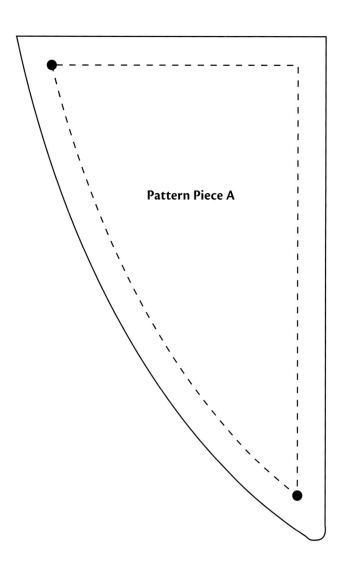

Pattern Piece A

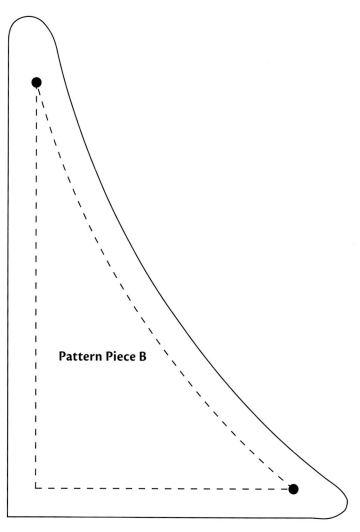

Pattern Piece B

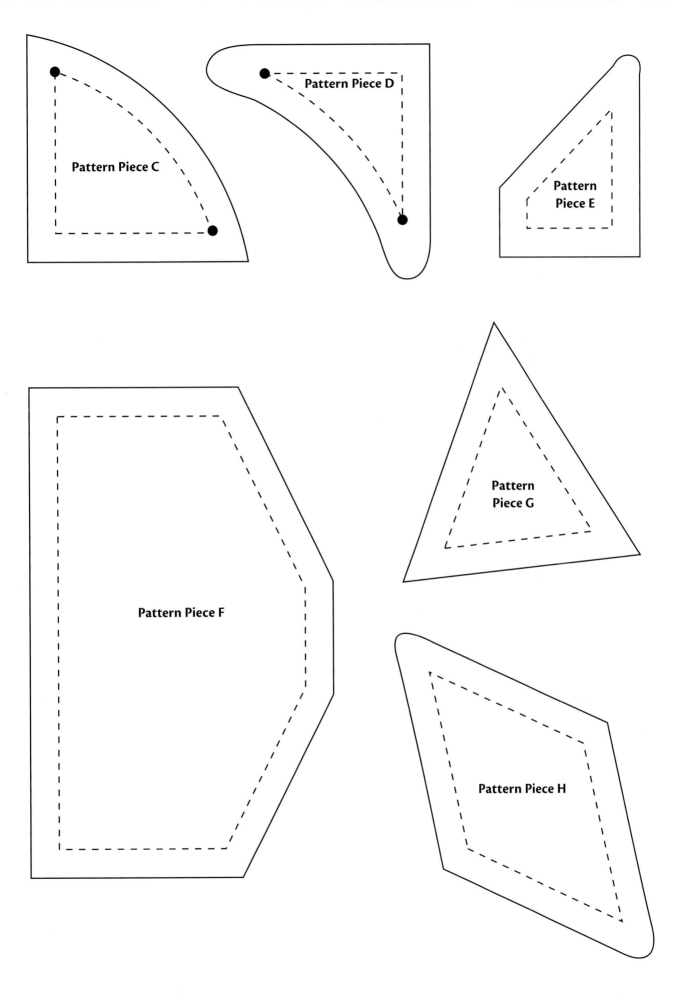

Pattern Piece C

Pattern Piece D

Pattern Piece E

Pattern Piece F

Pattern Piece G

Pattern Piece H

Four-Square Flowers

This design is based on a four-by-four grid pattern.
A few curved seams soften the appearance of what
would otherwise be a rigid layout.

Materials Needed

- ¼-yard brown print (flowers)
- ¼-yard gold print (flowers)
- ¼-yard yellow print (flowers)
- ¼-yard pale yellow (flowers)
- ¼-yard teal print (flowers)
- ¼-yard light blue print (flowers)
- ¼-yard purple print (flowers)
- ¼-yard lavender print (flowers)
- 1½ yards white-on-white print (flower centers and background)
- ½-yard lavender (sashing)
- ½-yard tan (sashing)
- 1 yard green (diamonds and triangles)
- 1½ yards green dot (border)
- ½-yard tan marble (border)
- 48" x 58" rectangle cotton fabric (backing)
- 48" x 58" rectangle cotton quilt batting
- 5¾ yards 2½"-wide bias binding or prepackaged double-fold bias binding
- 20 ivory buttons
- Green thread
- Coordinating thread
- 2 sheets 8½" x 11" tracing paper
- 2 sheets 8½" x 11" cardstock
- Air-soluble marking pen

Finished size: 46½" x 56"

The quilt top measures 47" x 56½" before quilting. The project will shrink slightly depending on the amount of quilting.

Seam allowances: ¼"

Templates: Use the templates on pages 31 and 32. Cut on the solid line and stitch on the broken line.

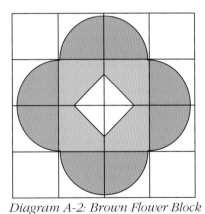

Cutting Plan

From the brown print, cut:
- 40 "A" shapes

From the gold print, cut:
- 20 "C" shapes

From the yellow print, cut:
- 40 "A" shapes

From the pale yellow, cut:
- 20 "C" shapes

From the teal print, cut:
- 40 "A" shapes

From the light blue print, cut:
- 20 "C" shapes

From the purple print, cut:
- 40 "A" shapes

From the lavender print, cut:
- 20 "C" shapes

From the lavender, cut:
- 40 2" x 7" strips

From the white-on-white print, cut:
- 160 "B" shapes
- 80 "D" shapes
- 80 2⅛" squares

From the tan, cut:
- 40 2" x 7" strips

From the green, cut:
- 12 4⅞" squares
- 14 "E" triangles
- four "F" triangles

From the green dot, cut:
- two 4¾" x 38" strips
- two 4¾" x 48" strips

From the tan marble, cut:
- four "G" triangles

Diagram A-1

Diagram A-2: Brown Flower Block

Diagram B-1

Diagram B-2: Yellow Flower Block

Make the Quilt Blocks

1 Match the curved shapes at the dots and stitch the brown print "A" shapes to the white "B" shapes, as in Diagram A-1. Refer to the instructions for Curved Patch Piecing on page 9 for assistance, if necessary. Press.

2 Stitch the gold print "C" shapes to the white "D" shapes. Press.

3 Stitch the squares from step 1, the squares from step 2 and four small white squares together to complete a 7" brown flower block, as in Diagram A-2. Press.

4 Repeat steps 1 through 3 to make a total of five brown flower blocks.

5 Repeat steps 1 through 4, but this time use the yellow print "A" shapes, white "B" shapes and the pale yellow "C" shapes, as shown in Diagram B-1, to complete five yellow flower blocks, as in Diagram B-2.

6 Repeat steps 1 through 4, but this time use the teal print "A" shapes, white "B" shapes and the light blue "C" shapes, as shown in Diagram C-1, to complete five teal flower blocks, as in Diagram C-2.

7 Repeat steps 1 through 4, but this time use the purple print "A" shapes, white "B" shapes and the lavender print "C" shapes, as shown in Diagram D-1, to complete five purple flower blocks, as in Diagram D-2.

Assemble the Quilt Top

1 Center and stitch the 2" x 7" tan strips to all four sides of each of the brown and the teal flower blocks. Press.

2 Stitch the 2" x 7" lavender strips to all four sides of each of the yellow and purple flower blocks. Press.

3 Use the marking pen to mark a diagonal line on the wrong side of each corner of each block, as shown in Diagram E-1, and trim excess fabric to within ¼" of the marked line.

4 Stitch the sides of four flower blocks together in a horizontal row, as shown in Diagram F-1, starting and stopping ¼" from each edge.

5 Refer to the Quilt Layout on the next page for color sequence and stitch the remaining flower blocks together for a total of five rows.

6 Review the instructions for Insetting Diagonal Pieces on page 9 and stitch the green diamonds and the triangles to the flower rows, as shown in Diagram G-1. Press.

7 Adjust the machine to a ⅛"-wide zigzag stitch and with the green thread, topstitch around the edges of the diamonds and the triangles.

8 Center and stitch the short green dot strips to the top and bottom of the quilt center. Press.

9 Stitch the long green dot strips to the sides of the quilt center. Press.

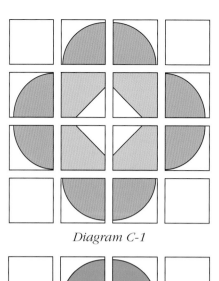

Diagram C-1

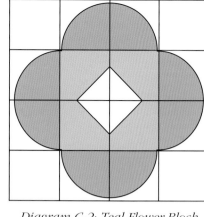

Diagram C-2: Teal Flower Block

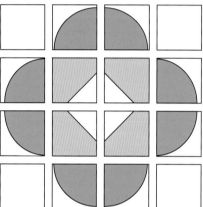

Diagram D-1

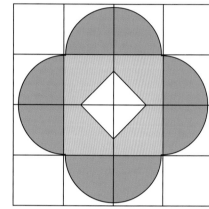

Diagram D-2: Purple Flower Block

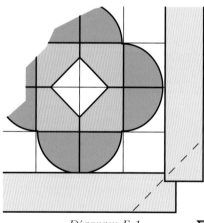

Diagram E-1

Diagram F-1

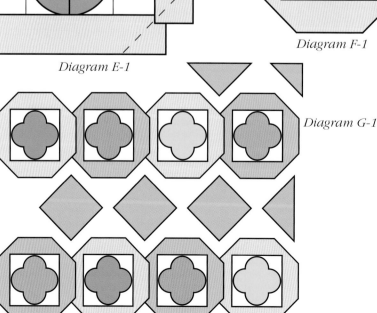

Diagram G-1

10 Mark a diagonal line on the wrong side of the quilt top at each corner, as shown in Diagram H-1.

12 Match the long sides of the tan marble triangles to the marked lines and stitch together to make the corners of the quilt top. Press.

11 Trim excess fabric to within ¼" of the marked lines.

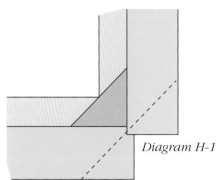

Diagram H-1

Quilt Layout

Finish the Quilt

1 Review the instructions for Marking the Quilt Top on page 11 and mark the quilting lines on the quilt top with the marking pen.

2 With the wrong side up, place the backing fabric on the work surface. Carefully smooth out any folds and center the batting on the top of the backing fabric.

3 With the right side up, center the quilt top on the batting.

4 Baste through all layers with pins or with long basting stitches, referring back to the Pinning and Basting section on page 11 for assistance, if necessary.

5 Review the Machine Quilting instructions on page 11 and machine quilt as desired.

6 Remove pins or basting stitches.

7 Trim the thread ends and then trim the edge of the quilt.

8 Stitch the bias binding around the edge of the quilt, as detailed in the Binding instructions on page 11.

9 Handstitch the buttons to the centers of the flowers.

The back of the quilt shows the detail of the machine quilting used for this particular design.

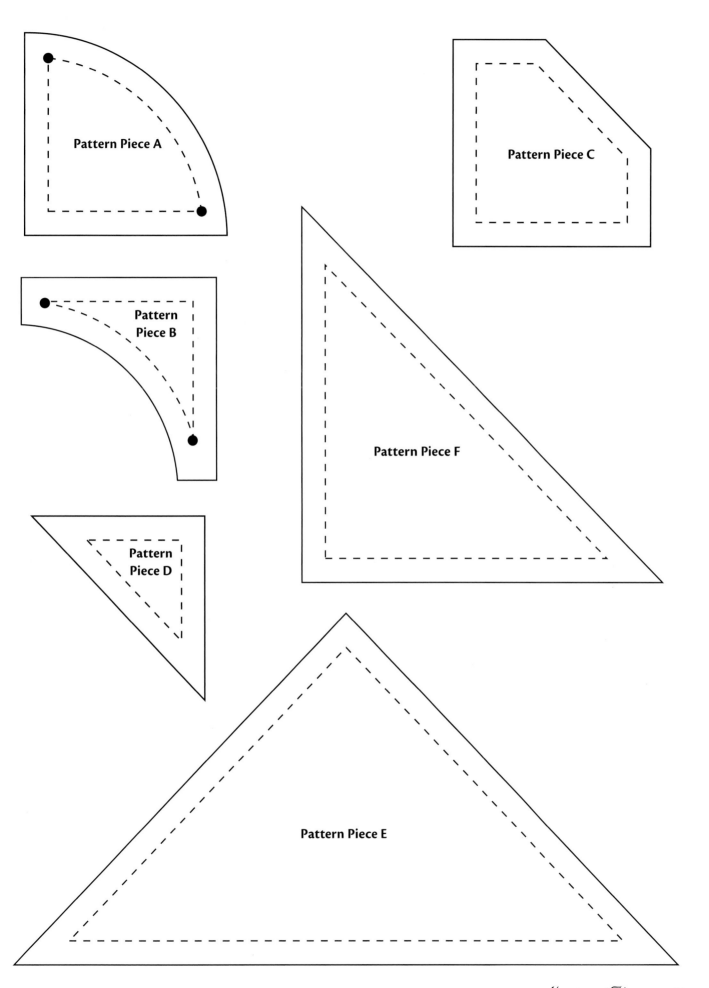

Pattern Piece A

Pattern Piece C

Pattern Piece B

Pattern Piece F

Pattern Piece D

Pattern Piece E

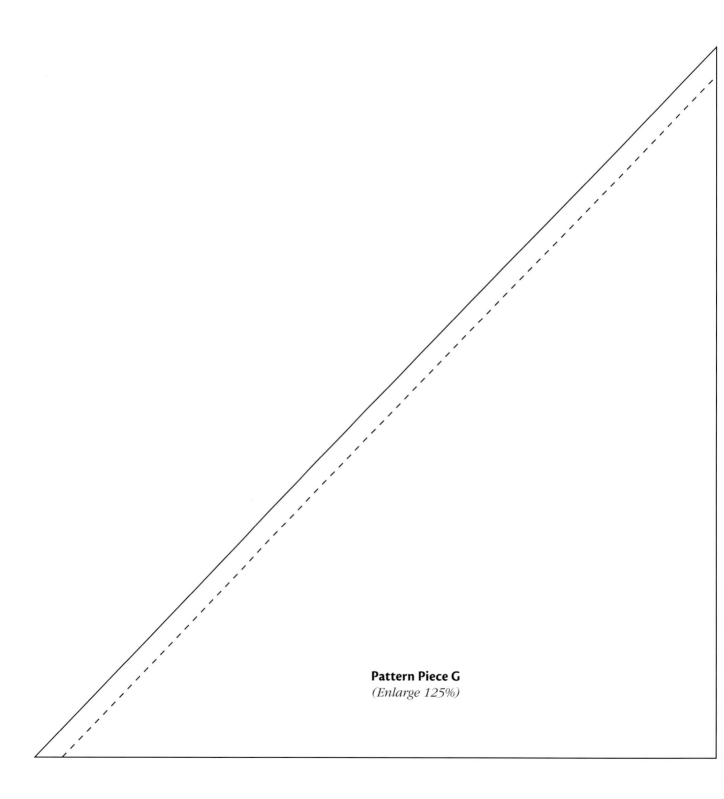

Pattern Piece G
(Enlarge 125%)

Whirligig Quince

Roses, tulips, poppies and poinsettias seem to be on everyone's list of favorite red flowers. This project celebrates the red quince, an overlooked but flashy flower of red.

Materials Needed

- 1 yard melon print (flowers)
- ¼-yard pastel stripe (flowers)
- 1 yard purple bull's-eye print (background)
- ½-yard turquoise print (background)
- 1 yard purple mosaic (background)
- 1½ yards yellow floral (background and border)
- 1½ yards blue print (border)
- 42" x 51" rectangle cotton fabric (backing)
- 42" x 51" rectangle cotton quilt batting
- 5½ yards 2½"-wide bias binding or prepackaged double-fold bias binding
- Coordinating thread
- ½-sheet 8½" x 11" tracing paper
- ½-sheet 8½" x 11" sheets cardstock
- Air-soluble marking pen

Finished size: 41" x 49¾"

The quilt measures 41½" x 50¼" before quilting. The project will shrink slightly depending upon the amount of quilting.

Seam allowances: ¼"

Templates: Use the templates on page 38. Cut on the solid line and stitch on the broken line.

Cutting Plan

From the melon print, cut:
- 80 "A" shapes

From the pastel stripe, cut:
- 20 1⅞" squares

From the purple bull's-eye print, cut:
- 80 "B" shapes

From the turquoise print, cut:
- 80 1½" x 3½" rectangles

From the purple mosaic, cut:
- 20 2½" x 7½" strips

From the yellow floral, cut:
- two 1½" x 45½" strips (Cut these long strips first.)
- two 1½" x 37½" strips
- 20 2½" x 7½" strips (Cut these short strips last.)

From the blue print, cut:
- two 2¾" x 42" strips
- two 2¾" x 51" strips

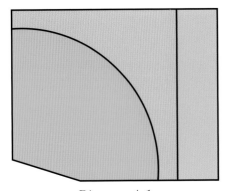

Diagram A-1

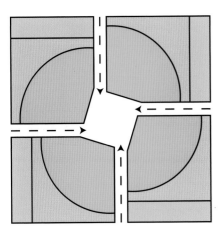

Diagram A-2

Make the Quilt Blocks

1 Match the curved shapes at the dots and stitch the melon "A" shapes to the purple print "B" shapes. Refer to the instructions for Curved Patch Piecing on page 9 for assistance, if necessary. Press.

2 Stitch the turquoise print rectangles to the right side of the "AB" squares, as in Diagram A-1. Press.

3 Place four of the pieced rectangles on the work surface and stitch the sides together, working toward the center and stopping ¼" from the center edge, as shown in Diagram A-2.

4 Review the instructions for Insetting Diagonal Pieces on page 9, match one side of one pastel square to one raw edge of an "A" shape and stitch together, starting and stopping ¼" from each edge.

5 Realign an adjoining side of the pastel square with the adjoining raw edge and stitch together.

6 Stitch the remaining two sides of the square to the remaining raw edges to complete. Press.

7 Repeat steps 3 through 6 to complete a total of 20 squares.

Assemble the Quilt Top

1 Center and stitch the purple mosaic print strips to the sides of each of the 20 pieced squares.

2 Center and stitch the short yellow floral strips to the sides of each of the 20 squares. Press.

3 Mark the wrong side of each square with the marking pen, as shown in Diagram B-1.

4 Trim excess fabric to within ¼" of the marked lines.

5 Alternating the background colors, stitch the squares together, referring to the Quilt Layout on the next page for placement. Press.

6 Center and stitch the 1½" x 37½" yellow floral strips to the top and the bottom of the quilt center, starting and stopping ¼" from each edge.

7 Stitch the 1½" x 45½" floral strips to the sides of the quilt.

8 Miter the corners, referring back to the instructions for Mitered Corners on page 10, if necessary. Press.

9 Center and stitch the 2¾" x 42" blue print strips to the top and the bottom of the quilt center, starting and stopping ¼" from each edge.

10 Stitch the 2¾" x 51" blue print strips to the sides of the quilt center, starting and stopping ¼" from each edge.

11 Miter the corners. Press.

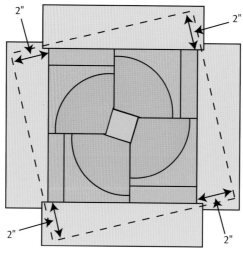

2" 2" 2" 2"

Diagram B-1

Finish the Quilt

1 Review the instructions for Marking the Quilt Top on page 11 and mark the quilting lines on the quilt top with the marking pen.

2 With the wrong side up, place the backing fabric on the work surface. Carefully smooth out any folds and center the batting on the top of the backing fabric.

3 With the right side up, center the quilt top on the batting.

4 Baste through all layers with pins or with long basting stitches, referring back to the Pinning and Basting section on page 11 for assistance, if necessary.

5 Review the Machine Quilting instructions on page 11 and machine quilt as desired.

6 Remove pins or basting stitches.

7 Trim the thread ends and then trim the edge of the quilt.

8 Stitch the bias binding around the edge of the quilt, as detailed in the Binding instructions on page 11.

The back of the quilt shows the detail of the machine quilting used for this particular design.

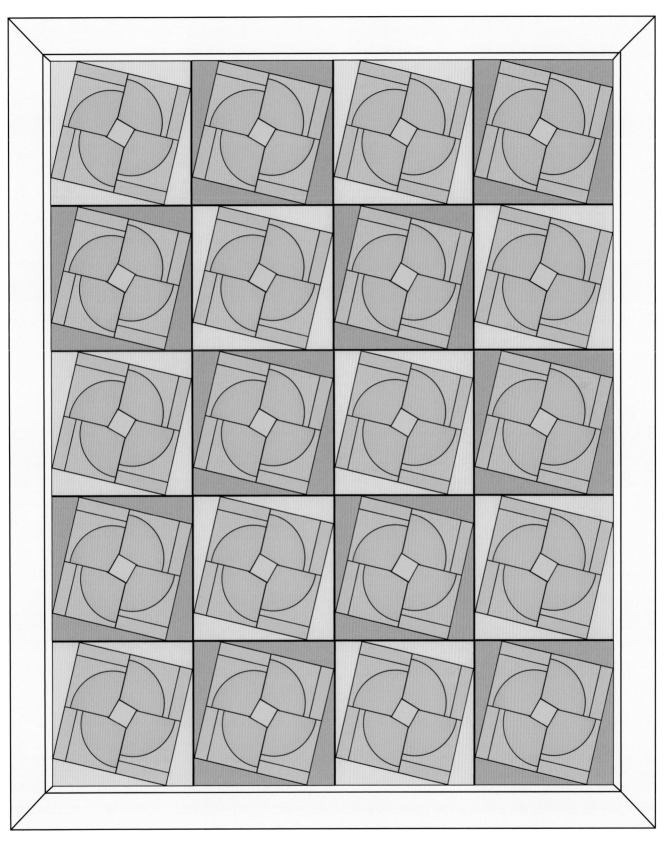

Quilt Layout

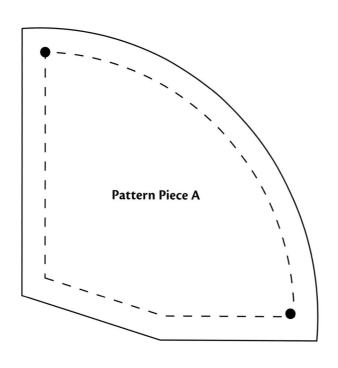

Pattern Piece A

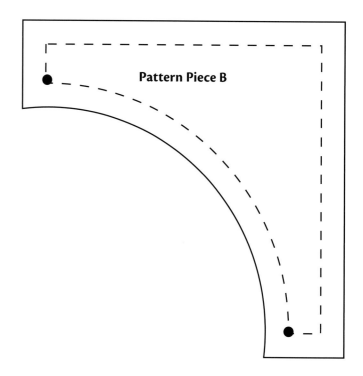

Pattern Piece B

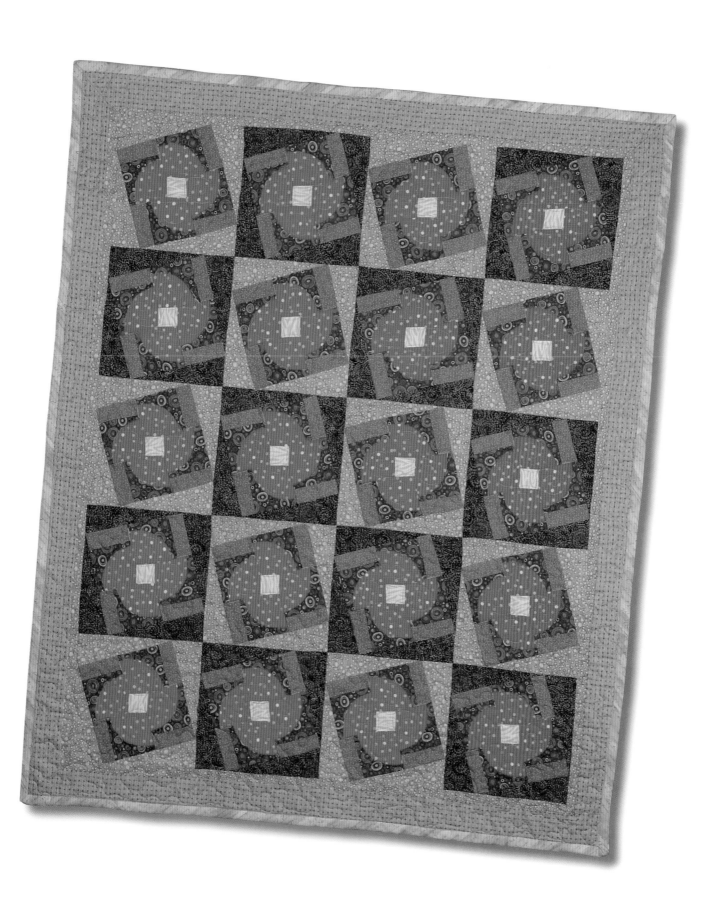

grace and movement

Blowing in the Wind

Adding curved lines to otherwise stiff formats helps to suggest grace and movement. The images assembled in this chapter are animated by curved seams and a gentle breeze.

Toy Boat, Toy Boat

This piece is the perfect wall hanging for boys of any age.
The trimmed sails serve as a breath of fresh air and bring a
salty feel to a favorite nook.

Materials Needed

- ¼-yard white-on-white print (boats)
- ⅛-yard red print (boats)
- 1¼ yards blue print (boat background, border and border corners)
- ⅓-yard rust print (boat background)
- ⅓-yard tan print (sashing)
- ¼-yard light blue (border corners)
- ⅛-yard medium blue (border corners)
- ⅛-yard turquoise print (border corners)
- 32" x 38" rectangle cotton fabric (backing)
- 32" x 38" rectangle cotton quilt batting
- 4 yards 2½"-wide bias binding or prepackaged double-fold bias binding
- Coordinating thread
- 2½ sheets 8½" x 11" tracing paper
- 2½ sheets 8½" x 11" cardstock
- Air-soluble marking pen

Finished size: 30½" x 37"

The quilt top measures 31" x 37½" before quilting. The project will shrink slightly depending on the amount of quilting.

Seam allowances: ¼"

Templates: Use the templates on pages 47 through 49. Cut on the solid line and stitch on the broken line.

Cutting Plan

From the white-on-white print, cut:
- four "A" shapes
- four "B" shapes

From the red print, cut:
- four "C" shapes

From the blue print, cut:
- four "D" shapes
- four "E" shapes
- four "F" shapes
- four "G" shapes
- four "H" shapes
- four reverse "H" shapes
- 16 "I" shapes
- two 5¾" x 20½" strips
- two 5¾" x 25" strips

From the rust print, cut:
- eight 2" x 7½" strips
- eight 2" x 14" strips

From the tan print, cut:
- two 2" x 11½" strips
- one 2" x 17½" strip
- two 2" x 20½" strips
- two 2" x 27" strips

From the light blue, cut:
- 16 "J" shapes

From the medium blue, cut:
- eight "K" shapes

From the turquoise print, cut:
- eight "K" shapes

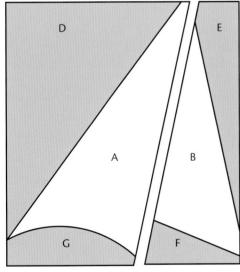

Diagram A-1   Diagram A-2

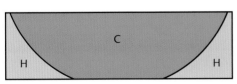

Diagram A-3

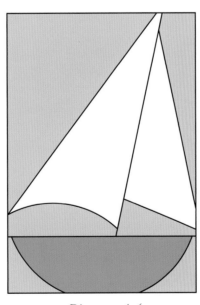

Diagram A-4

Make the Quilt Blocks

1 Match the curved shapes at the dots and stitch one white "A" shape, one blue print "D" shape and one blue print "G" shape together, as in Diagram A-1. Review the instructions for Curved Patch Piecing on page 9, if necessary. Press.

2 Stitch one white "B" shape, one "E" shape and one blue print "F" shape together, as in Diagram A-2. Press.

3 Stitch one pair of "H" shapes to one "C" shape, as in Diagram A-3. Press.

4 Stitch the three pieced sections together to make one boat block, as shown in Diagram A-4. Press.

5 Center and stitch two 2" x 7½" rust print strips to the top and the bottom of one boat block. Press.

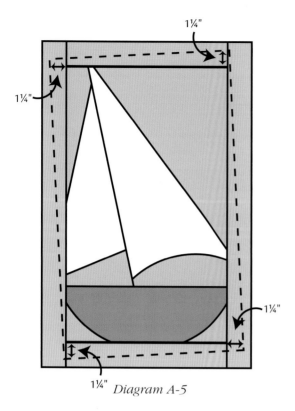

1¼"

1¼"

1¼"

1¼"

1¼"

Diagram A-5

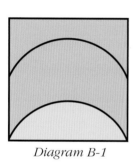

Diagram B-1

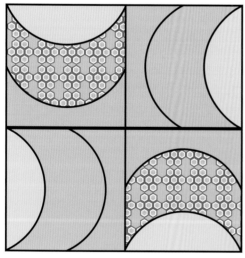

Diagram B-2

6 Center and stitch two 2" x 14" rust print strips to the sides of the boat block. Press.

7 Repeat steps 1 through 6 to make a total of four complete blocks.

8 Mark the wrong sides of the blocks with the marking pen, as in Diagram A-5, and trim excess fabric to within ¼" of the marked lines.

9 Stitch together one blue print "I" shape, one light blue "J" shape and one medium blue "K" shape, as shown in Diagram B-1. Press.

10 Repeat step 9 to make a total of 16 squares, but on eight of the squares, use the turquoise "K" shapes in place of the medium blue.

11 Stitch four squares together to make a large square, as in Diagram B-2.

12 Repeat step 11 to make a total of four large squares. These are the border corners.

Assemble the Quilt Top

1 Stitch together the boat blocks, two 2" x 11½" tan print strips and one 2" x 17½" tan print strip, referring to the Quilt Layout on the next page for placement assistance. Press.

2 Center and stitch the 2" x 20½" tan print strips to the top and the bottom of the quilt center, starting and stopping ¼" from each edge.

3 Stitch the 2" x 27" tan print strips to the sides of the quilt center, starting and stopping ¼" from each edge. Press.

4 Miter the corners, as detailed in the instructions for Mitered Corners on page 10. Press.

5 Stitch the 5¾" x 20½" blue print strips to the top and the bottom of the quilt center. Press.

6 Stitch the pieced border corners to the ends of the 2" x 27" blue print strips. Press.

7 Stitch the pieced strips created in step 6 to the sides of the quilt center. Press.

Finish the Quilt

1 Review the instructions for Marking the Quilt Top on page 11 and mark the quilting lines on the quilt top with the marking pen.

2 With the wrong side up, place the backing fabric on the work surface. Carefully smooth out any folds and center the batting on the top of the backing fabric.

3 With the right side up, center the quilt top on the batting.

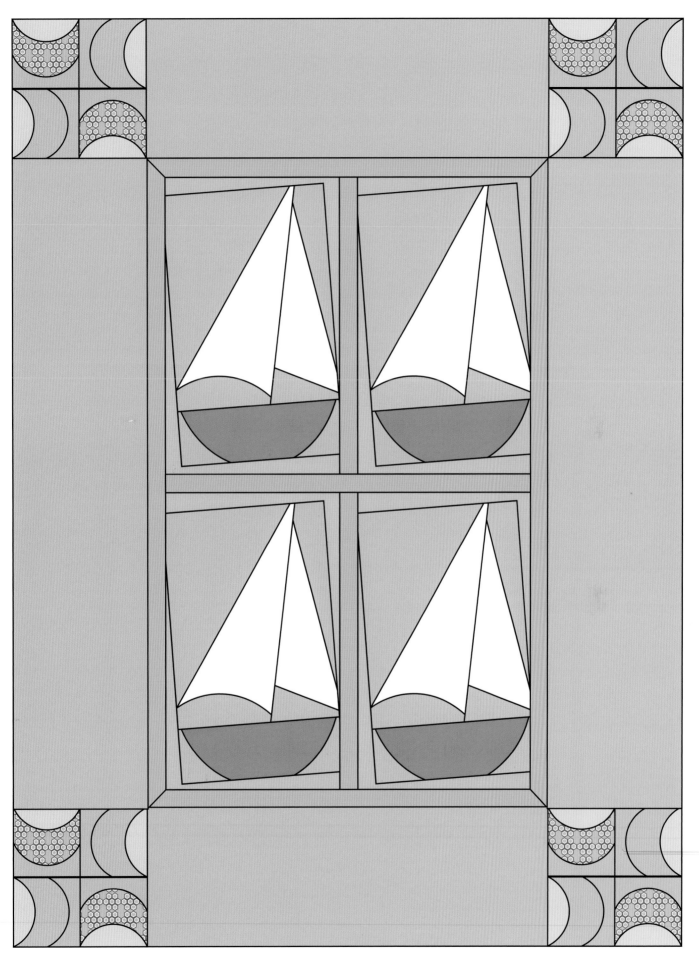

Quilt Layout

4 Baste through all layers with pins or with long basting stitches, referring back to the Pinning and Basting section on page 11 for assistance, if necessary.

5 Review the Machine Quilting instructions on page 11 and machine quilt as desired.

6 Remove pins or basting stitches.

7 Trim the thread ends and then trim the edge of the quilt.

8 Stitch the bias binding around the edge of the quilt, as detailed in the Binding instructions on page 11.

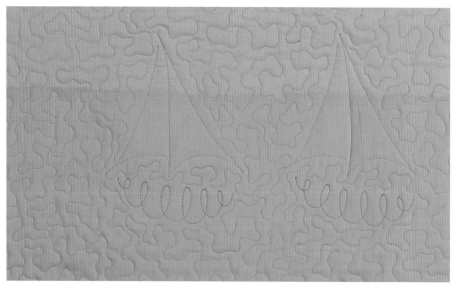

The back of the quilt shows the detail of the machine quilting used for this particular design.

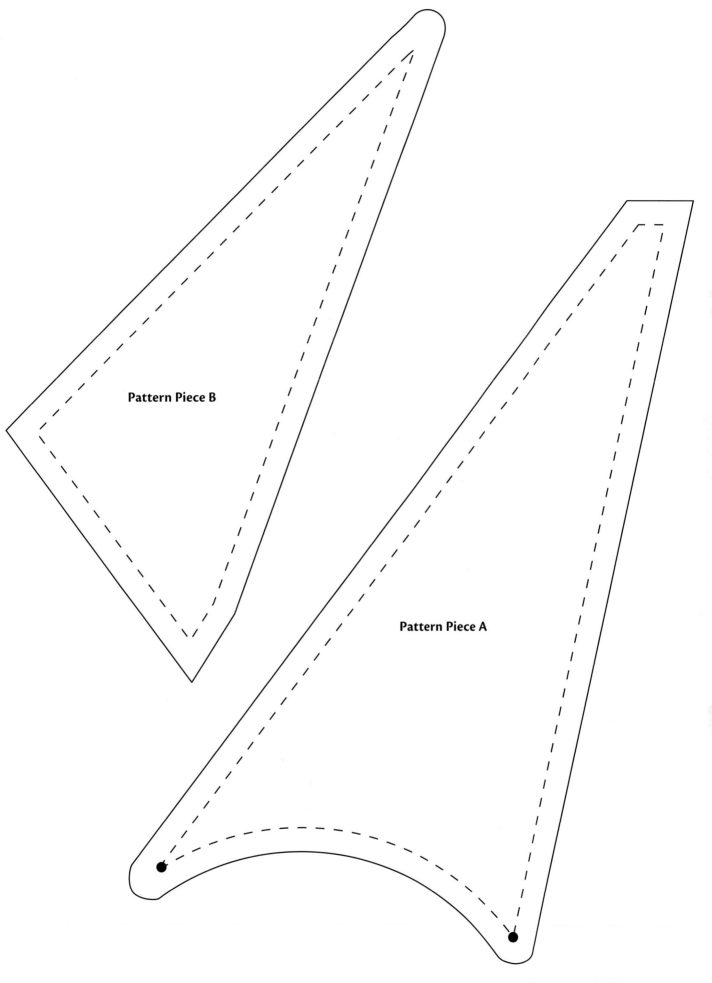

Pattern Piece B

Pattern Piece A

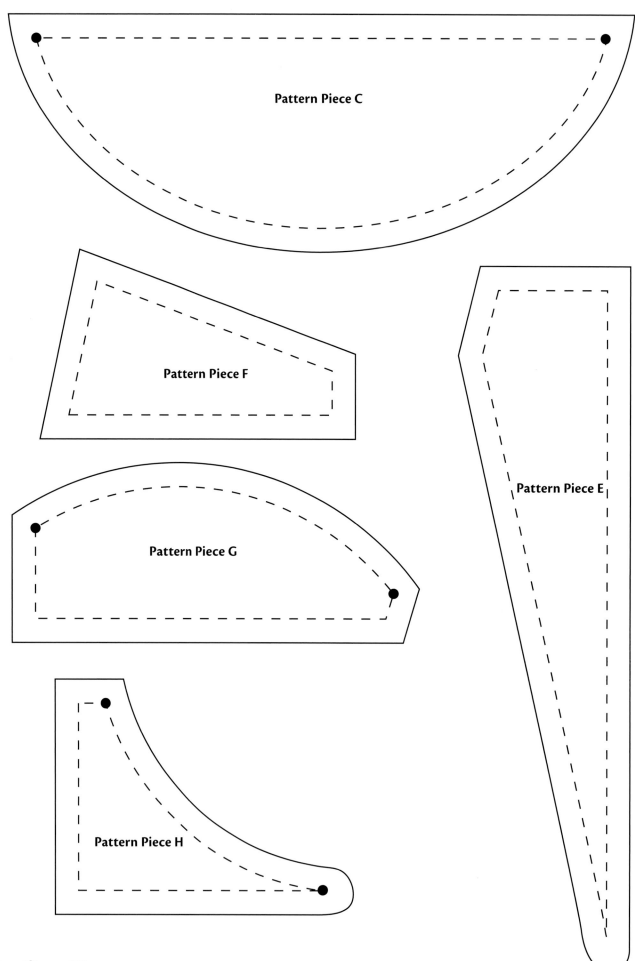

Pattern Piece C

Pattern Piece F

Pattern Piece E

Pattern Piece G

Pattern Piece H

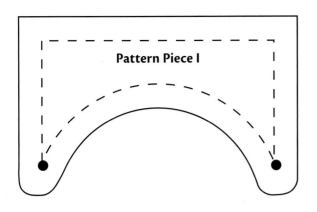

Pattern Piece I

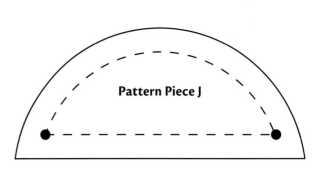

Pattern Piece J

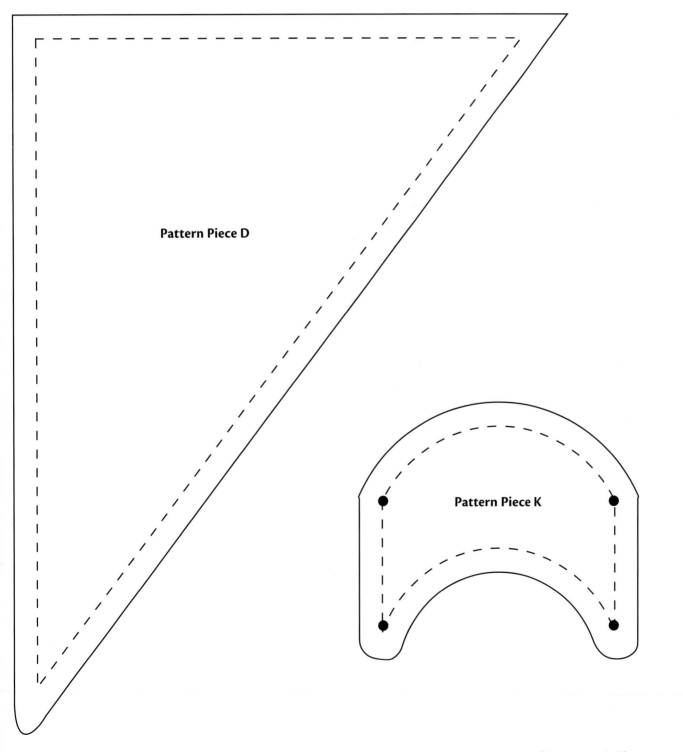

Pattern Piece D

Pattern Piece K

Falling Leaves

Refer to the quilt layout to arrange these blocks, or stir them
around to create a windswept random arrangement. Choose
contrasting fabrics for blank blocks to achieve a more graphic look.

Materials Needed

- ¼-yard red print (red leaves)
- ¼-yard rust print (red leaves)
- 1/8-yard purple mosaic (green leaves)
- 1/8-yard light green print (green leaves)
- ¼-yard olive print (green leaves)
- 1 yard gold print (leaf background)
- ¼-yard each of four coordinating prints (remaining squares)
- ¼-yard brown stripe (border)
- ½-yard olive crackle (border)
- 40" x 45" rectangle cotton fabric (backing)
- 40" x 45" rectangle cotton quilt batting
- 4¾ yards 2½"-wide bias binding or prepackaged double-fold bias binding
- 2 skeins green embroidery floss
- 2 skeins brown embroidery floss
- Coordinating thread
- 1 sheet 8½" x 11" tracing paper
- 1 sheet 8½" x 11" cardstock
- Air-soluble marking pen

Finished size: 38½" x 43½"

The quilt top measures 39" x 44" before quilting. The project will shrink slightly depending on the amount of quilting.

Seam allowances: ¼"

Templates: Use the templates on page 55. Cut on the solid line and stitch on the broken line.

Cutting Plan

From the red print, cut:
- 24 "A" triangles
- 12 1¾" squares
- 12 "B" shapes

From the rust print, cut:
- 24 "A" triangles
- 12 "B" shapes

From the purple mosaic, cut:
- 10 "D" shapes

From the light green print, cut:
- 10 ¾" x 16" strips

From the olive print, cut:
- 10 ¾" x 8" strips
- 20 "E" shapes

From the gold print, cut:
- 88 "A" triangles
- 12 1¾" x 4¼" strips
- 12 1¾" x 5½" strips
- 20 "F" shapes
- 10 3" squares

From the coordinating fabrics, cut:
- a total of 20 5½" squares

From the brown stripe, cut:
- two 2" x 33½" strips
- two 2" x 38½" strips

From the olive crackle, cut:
- four 3½" x 39" strips

Red Print

Rust Print

Gold Print

Diagram A-1

*Diagram A-2:
Red Leaf Square*

Diagram B-1

Diagram B-2

Make the Quilt Blocks

1 Match the curved shapes at the dots and stitch the specified leaf shapes together to make one "BC" square and four "AA" squares, as shown in Diagram A-1 and its accompanying color code. Review the instructions for Curved Patch Piecing on page 9 for assistance, if necessary. Press.

2 Stitch the pieced squares from step 1 together with one red print square, one 1¾" x 4¼" gold print strip and one 1¾" x 5½" gold print strip to make a 5½" square, as shown in Diagram A-2. Press.

3 Repeat steps 1 and 2 to make a total of 12 red leaf squares.

4 Cut eight 2" lengths from the ¾" x 16" light green print strips.

5 Stitch four of the ¾" x 2" light green strips created in step 4 to one purple mosaic "D" shape, as in Diagram B-1. Press.

6 Rotate the "D" shape and overlapping the first row, stitch four more strips to the "D" shape, as in Diagram B-2. Press.

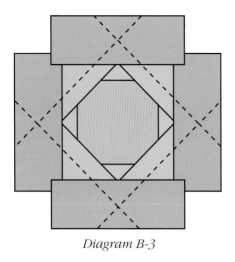

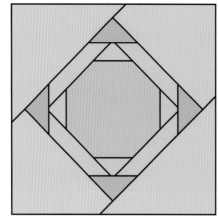

Diagram B-3

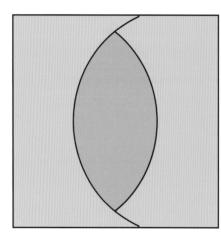

Diagram B-4: Diamond Square

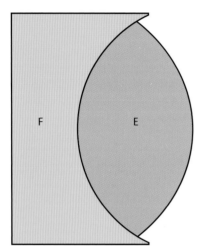

F

E

Diagram C-1

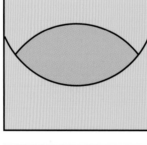

Diagram C-2: Green Leaf Square

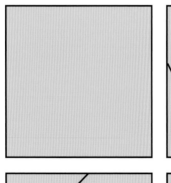

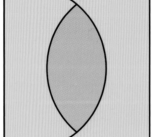

Diagram D-1: Diamond Leaf Square

7 Cut four 2" lengths from one ¾" x 8" olive strip.

8 Rotate the pieced section from step 6 again and stitch the newly created ¾" x 2" olive strips to the light green strips, as in Diagram B-3. Press.

9 Mark the diagonal stitching lines on the wrong side of the step 8 pieced shape and stitch four gold print triangles to the pieced shape and trim excess fabric from the green print strips to make a 3" square, as in Diagram B-4. Press.

10 Repeat steps 5 through 9 to make a total of 10 diamond squares.

11 Stitch an "F" shape to one side of an "E" leaf, matching the curves, as in Diagram C-1.

12 Stitch the other "F" shape to the other side of the pieced "E" leaf and trim the excess fabric to create a leaf square, as in Diagram C-2.

13 Repeat steps 11 and 12 to make a total of 20 green leaf squares.

14 Stitch together one diamond square, two green leaf squares and one gold print square, as in Diagram D-1. Press.

15 Repeat step 1 to make a total of 10 pieced diamond-leaf squares.

Assemble the Quilt Top

1 Stitch the red leaf squares, the diamond-leaf squares and the coordinating fabric squares together, as shown in the Quilt Layout on on the next page. Press.

2 Center and stitch the 2" x 33½" brown stripe strips to the top and the bottom of the quilt center, starting and stopping ¼" from each edge. Press.

3 Stitch the 2" x 38½" brown stripe strips to the sides of the quilt center, starting and stopping ¼" from each edge. Press.

4 Miter the corners, as detailed in the instructions for Mitered Corners on page 10. Press.

5 Stitch two green crackle strips to the sides of the quilt center. Press.

6 Stitch the remaining green crackle strips to the top and the bottom of the quilt center. Press.

7 Mark the stems with the marking pen, as shown in Diagrams E-1 and E-2.

8 Review the Hand-Embroidery instructions on page 10 and use three strands of brown floss to embroider the stems on the red leaf squares with a wrapped backstitch.

9 Use three strands of green floss to embroider the stems on the diamond-leaf squares with a wrapped backstitch.

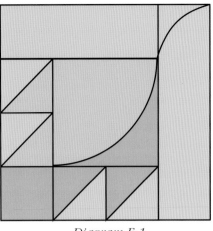

Diagram E-1

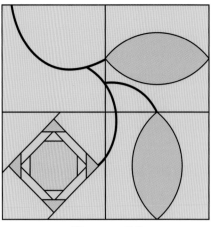

Diagram E-2

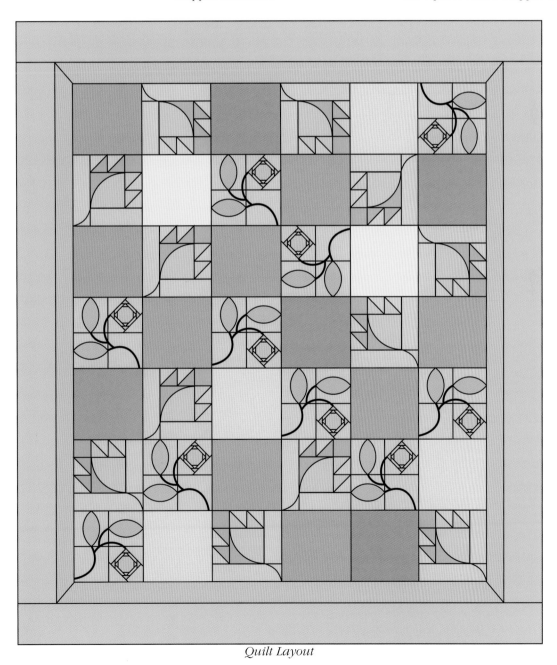

Quilt Layout

*The back of the quilt shows
the detail of the machine quilting
used for this particular design.*

Finish the Quilt

1 Review the instructions for Marking the Quilt Top on page 11 and mark the quilting lines on the quilt top with the marking pen.

2 With the wrong side up, place the backing fabric on the work surface. Carefully smooth out any folds and center the batting on the top of the backing fabric.

3 With the right side up, center the quilt top on the batting.

4 Baste through all layers with pins or with long basting stitches, referring back to the Pinning and Basting section on page 11 for assistance, if necessary.

5 Review the Machine Quilting instructions on page 11 and machine quilt as desired.

6 Remove pins or basting stitches.

7 Trim the thread ends and then trim the edge of the quilt.

8 Stitch the bias binding around the edge of the quilt, as detailed in the Binding instructions on page 11.

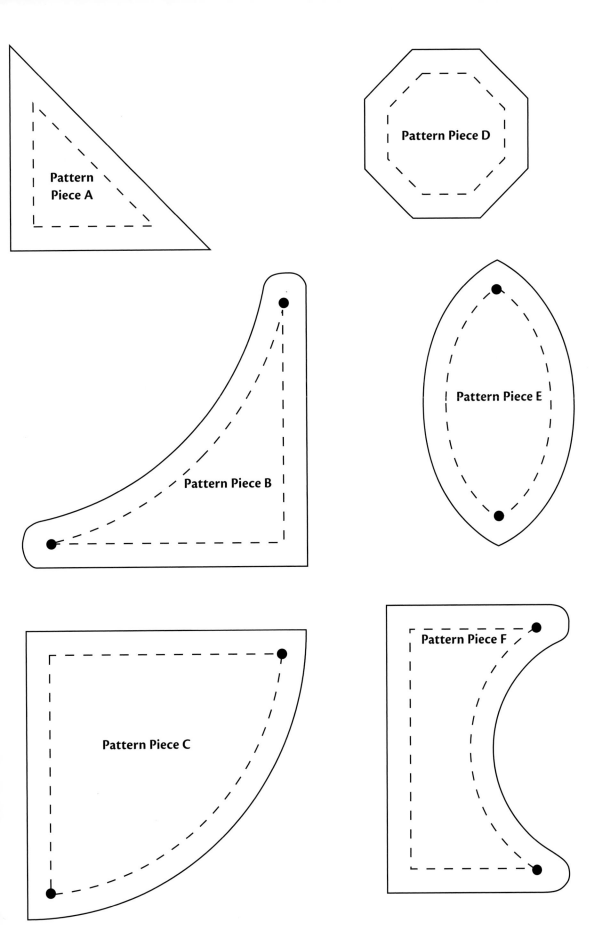

Pattern Piece A

Pattern Piece D

Pattern Piece B

Pattern Piece E

Pattern Piece C

Pattern Piece F

Pinwheels and Ribbons

Pinwheels and Ribbons

Graceful blue ribbons dance between rows of pinwheels in
this design. To make the rows distinct, complementary colors
of orange and blue are used in the color palette.

Materials Needed

- ½-yard peach (pinwheels)
- ½-yard peach print (pinwheels)
- ½-yard taupe (pinwheels)
- ¾-yard taupe print
  (pinwheels and border)
- ½-yard blue (ribbons)
- ¾-yard blue print (ribbons)
- 1½ yards muslin (background)
- ½-yard tan print (border)
- ¼-yard multi-umbrella print (border)
- 51" square cotton fabric (backing)
- 51" square cotton quilt batting
- 5¾ yards 2½"-wide bias binding or
  prepackaged double-fold bias binding
- Coordinating thread
- 1 sheet 8½" x 11" tracing paper
- 1 sheet 8½" x 11" cardstock
- Air-soluble marking pen

Finished size: 48½" square

The quilt top measures 49¼" square before quilting. The project will shrink slightly depending on the amount of quilting.

Seam allowances: ¼"

Templates: Use the templates on page 60. Cut on the solid line and stitch on the broken line.

Cutting Plan

From the peach, cut:
- 50 "A" triangles

From the peach print, cut:
- 50 "A" triangles

From the taupe, cut:
- 50 "A" triangles

From the taupe print, cut:
- 50 "A" triangles
- four 1¾" x 39½" strips

From the blue, cut:
- 50 "D" shapes

From the blue print, cut:
- 100 "C" triangles

From the muslin, cut:
- 50 "B" triangles
- 50 "E" shapes

From the tan print, cut:
- four 4¼" x 39½" strips

From the multi-umbrella print, cut:
- four 5½" squares

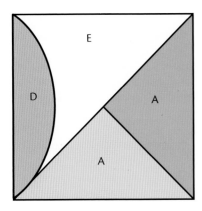

Diagram A-1

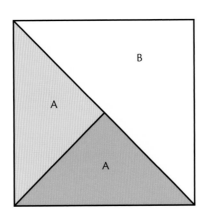

Diagram B-1

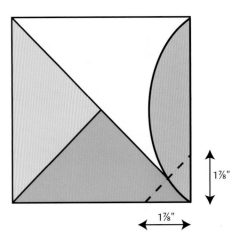

1⅞"

1⅞"

Diagram C-1

Make the Quilt Blocks

1 Match the curved shapes at the dots and stitch the blue "D" shapes to the muslin "E" shapes. Review the instructions for Curved Patch Piecing on page 9 for assistance, if necessary. Press.

2 Stitch one peach "A" triangle, one peach print "A" triangle and one pieced triangle from step 1 together to form a square, as shown in Diagram A-1. Press.

3 Repeat to make a total of 25 squares.

4 Stitch one peach "A" triangle, one peach print "A" triangle and one muslin "B" triangle together to form a square, as in Diagram B-1. Press.

5 Repeat step 4 to make a total of 25 squares.

6 Repeat steps 1 through 5 with the taupe and taupe print "A" triangles to make 25 "A" squares and 25 "B" squares.

7 Use the marking pen to mark a diagonal line at the corner on the wrong side of one "A" square, as in Diagram C-1.

8 Trim excess fabric to within ¼" of the marked line.

9 Match the long side of a blue print triangle to the marked line on the "A" square and stitch the two together. Press.

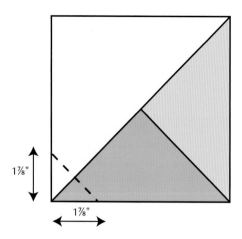

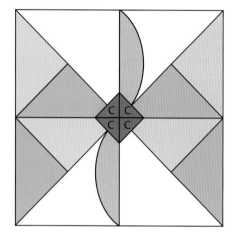

Diagram D-1

Diagram E-1

11 Mark a diagonal line at the corner on the wrong side of one "B" square, as shown in Diagram D-1.

12 Trim the excess fabric to within ¼" of the marked line.

13 Match a blue print triangle to the marked line on the "B" square and stitch the two together. Press.

14 Repeat steps 11 through 13 with the remaining "B" squares.

Assemble the Quilt Top

1 Stitch two pieced "A" squares and two pieced "B" squares together, as shown in Diagram E-1. Press.

2 Repeat step 1 to make a total of 25 pieced squares. Press.

3 Stitch the pieced squares together, as shown in the Quilt Layout on the next page to make the quilt center. Press.

4 Stitch the long sides of the 1¾" x 39½" taupe print strips to the long sides of the 4¼" x 39½" tan print strips. Press.

5 With the taupe print strips as the inner border, center and stitch two step 4 pieced strips to the sides of the quilt center. Press.

6 Stitch the multi-umbrella squares to the short ends of the remaining pieced strips. Press.

7 Stitch the remaining taupe-tan print strips to the top and bottom of the quilt center. Press.

Finish the Quilt

1 Review the instructions for Marking the Quilt Top on page 11 and mark the quilting lines on the quilt top with the marking pen.

2 With the wrong side up, place the backing fabric on the work surface. Carefully smooth out any folds and center the batting on the top of the backing fabric.

3 With the right side up, center the quilt top on the batting.

4 Baste through all layers with pins or with long basting stitches, referring back to the Pinning and Basting section on page 11 for assistance, if necessary.

5 Review the Machine Quilting instructions on page 11 and machine quilt as desired.

6 Remove pins or basting stitches.

7 Trim the thread ends and then trim the edge of the quilt.

8 Stitch the bias binding around the edge of the quilt, as detailed in the Binding instructions on page 11.

10 Repeat steps 7 through 9 with the remaining "A" squares.

The back of the quilt shows the detail of the machine quilting used for this particular design.

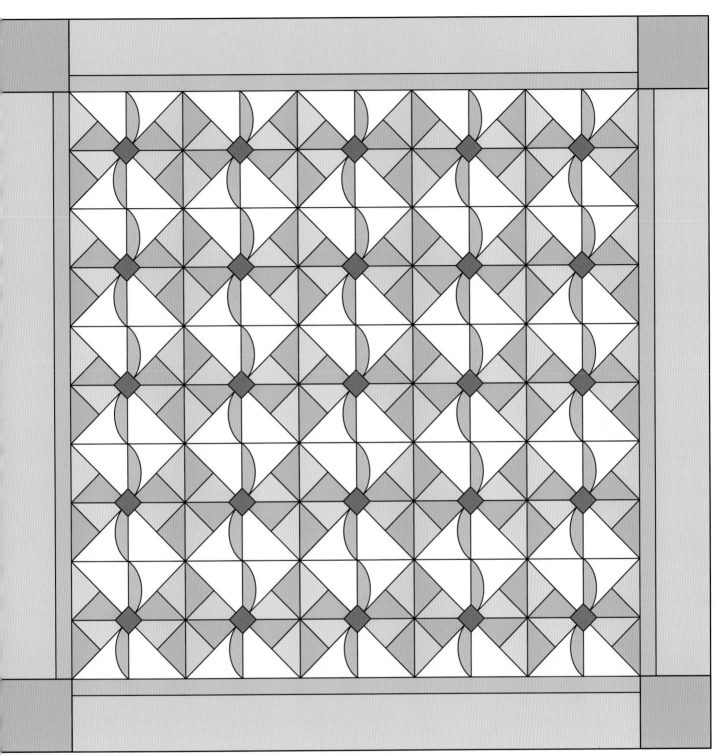

Quilt Layout

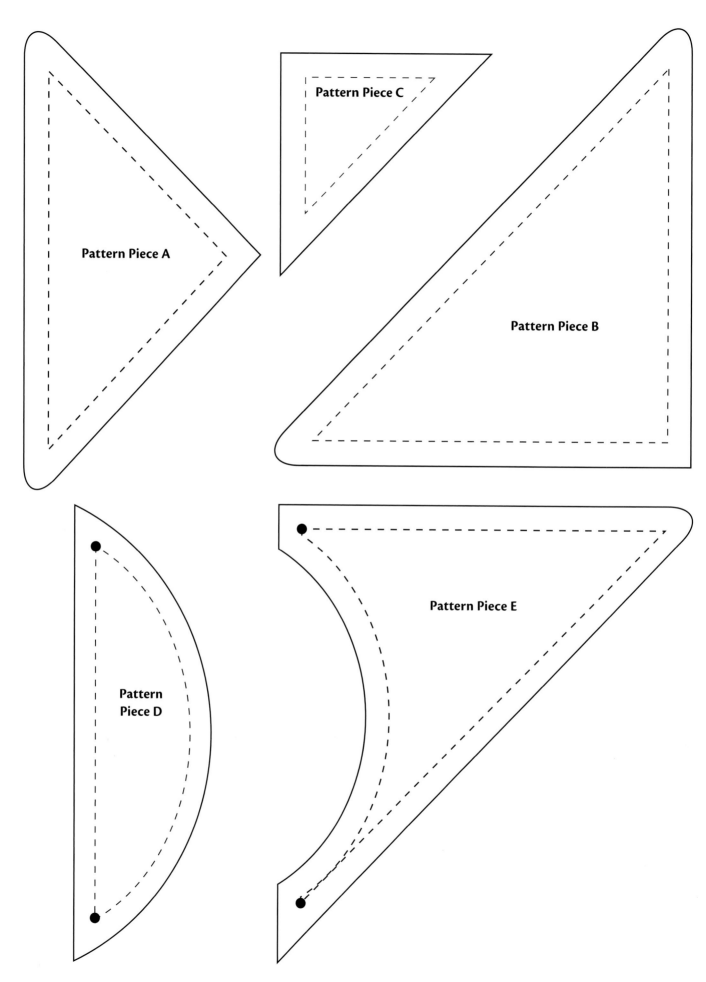

Pattern Piece A

Pattern Piece C

Pattern Piece B

Pattern Piece D

Pattern Piece E

Trippy Butterflies

Choose fabrics for butterfly wings that coordinate, rather than match.
Coordinating colors and patterns are close in appearance, but not the same.
When combined, they have a flow that keeps your eye moving around the quilt surface.

Materials Needed

- ¼-yard peach mini-dot (butterflies)
- ¼-yard dark pink mottle (butterflies)
- ¼-yard pink feather print (butterflies)
- ¼-yard burgundy (butterflies)
- ¼-yard dark pink leaf print (butterflies)
- ¼-yard lavender print (butterflies)
- ⅛-yard peach print (butterflies)
- ⅛-yard red (butterflies)
- ⅛-yard light pink mottle (butterflies)
- ⅛-yard peach (butterflies)
- 1 yard pale yellow (butterfly background)
- ¼-yard cream rain print (sashing)
- 1 yard taupe floral print (sashing)
- ⅛-yard purple floral print (sashing)
- ½-yard pink geometric print (border)
- ⅛-yard tan print (border corners)
- 39" x 51" rectangle cotton fabric (backing)
- 39" x 51" rectangle cotton quilt batting
- 5 yards 2½"-wide bias binding or prepackaged double-fold bias binding
- 9" x 12" piece brown felt
- ½-yard lightweight tear-away stabilizer for machine embroidery
- Brown thread
- Coordinating thread
- 1 sheet 8½" x 11" tracing paper
- 1 sheet 8½" x 11" cardstock
- Air-soluble marking pen

Finished size: 37" x 49"

The quilt top measures 38" x 50" before quilting. The project will shrink slightly depending on the amount of quilting.

Seam allowances: ¼"

Templates: Use the templates on page 67. Cut on the solid line and stitch on the broken line.

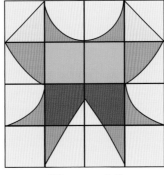

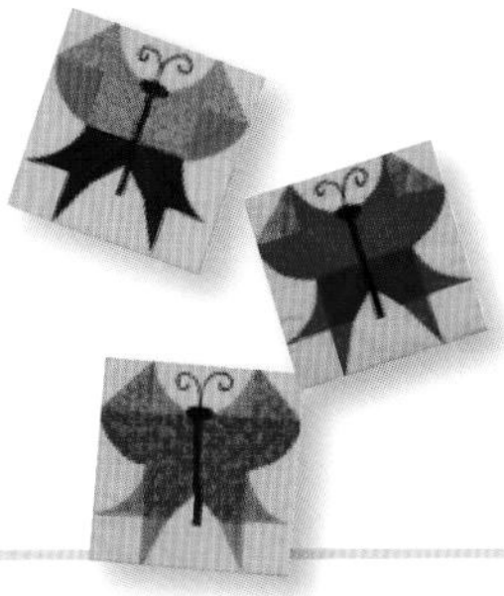

Cutting Plan

From the peach mini-dot, cut:
- 24 "A" shapes
- four "E" triangles
- four reverse "E" triangles

From the dark pink mottle, cut:
- eight "A" shapes
- eight 2½" squares
- four "E" triangles
- four reverse "E" triangles

From the pink feather print, cut:
- eight "B" shapes
- eight "C" shapes
- eight 2½" squares

From the burgundy, cut:
- eight "A" shapes
- eight "C" shapes
- four "E" triangles
- four reverse "E" triangles

From the dark pink leaf print, cut:
- eight "A" shapes
- eight "B" shapes

From the peach print, cut:
- eight "G" triangles

From the red, cut:
- eight "C" shapes

From the light pink mottle, cut:
- eight "G" triangles

From the peach, cut:
- eight "B" shapes

From the lavender print, cut:
- eight "G" triangles
- eight 2½" squares

From the pale yellow, cut:
- 32 "A" shapes
- 64 "B" shapes
- 32 "D" shapes
- 32 "G" shapes
- 32 2½" squares
- 16 "F" shapes
- 16 reverse "F" shapes

From the brown felt, cut:
- 16 "H" shapes

From the cream rain print, cut:
- six 4½" squares

From the taupe floral print, cut:
- 34 2¼" x 8½" rectangles
- two 1¾" x 18" strips
- two 2½" x 18" strips

From the purple floral print, cut:
- three 1" x 18" strips

From the pink geometric print cut:
- two 3½" x 32½" strips
- two 3½" x 44½" strips

From the tan print, cut:
- four 3½" squares

From stabilizer, cut:
- 12 3" x 7" rectangles

Make the Quilt Blocks

1 Match the curved shapes at the dots and stitch the specified butterfly shapes to the yellow background shapes, as shown in Diagram A-1 and its accompanying color code. Review the instructions for Curved Patch Piecing on page 9 for assistance, if necessary. Press.

2 Stitch the squares together as in Diagram A-2 to make an 8½" block. Press.

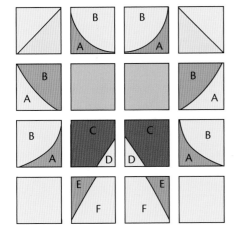

Peach Print   Dark PinkMottle   Pale Yellow

Dark Pink Leaf Print   Red

Diagram A-1

Diagram A-2:
"A" Butterfly Block

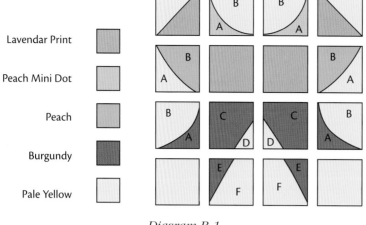

Lavendar Print

Peach Mini Dot

Peach

Burgundy

Pale Yellow

Diagram B-1

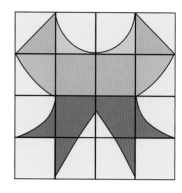

Diagram B-2:
"B" Butterfly Block

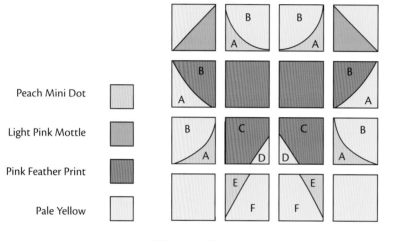

Peach Mini Dot

Light Pink Mottle

Pink Feather Print

Pale Yellow

Diagram C-1

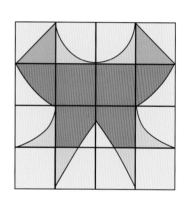

Diagram C-2:
"C" Butterfly Blocks

3 Repeat steps 1 and 2 to make a total of four "A" butterfly blocks.

4 Match the curved shapes at the dots and stitch the specified butterfly shapes to the yellow background shapes, as shown in Diagram B-1 and its accompanying color code.

5 Stitch the squares together as in Diagram B-2 to make an 8½" block. Press.

6 Repeat steps 4 and 5 to make a total of four "B" butterfly blocks.

7 Match the curved shapes at the dots and stitch the specified butterfly shapes to the yellow background shapes, as shown in Diagram C-1 and its accompanying color code.

8 Stitch the squares together as in Diagram C-2 to make an 8½" block. Press.

9 Repeat steps 4 and 5 to make a total of four "C" butterfly blocks.

10 Center and baste one "H" shape (body and antennae) on one pieced butterfly block with the head centered on the top horizontal seam and the body on the center seam.

11 Use the marking pen to mark the antennae above the head.

12 Pin one 3" x 7" stabilizer rectangle in place to the wrong side of the square behind the body and antennae.

13 On a scrap of fabric, machine satin stitch a short straight line. Adjust your machine to the desired line width and coverage. The width of the stitching line on the photo model is slightly wider than $\frac{1}{16}$".

14 With the brown thread, satin stitch around the felt and along the antennae lines and trim the thread ends.

15 Remove the basting stitches and carefully tear the stabilizer from the back of the square.

16 Repeat steps 10 through 15 for all of the remaining butterfly blocks.

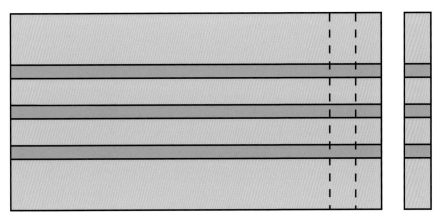

Diagram D-1

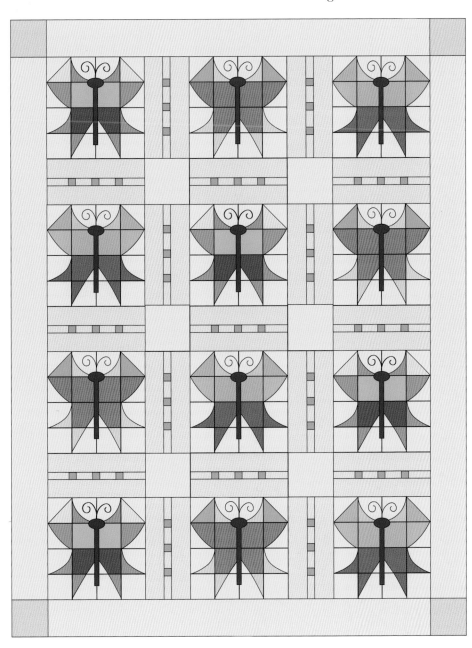

Quilt Layout

Assemble the Quilt Top

1 Stitch the 1" x 18" purple floral print strips between the 18" taupe floral strips, as shown in Diagram D-1. Press.

2 Cut 17 1"-wide strips perpendicular to the seam lines.

3 Stitch one pieced strip between two 2¼" x 8½" taupe floral rectangles to make a 4½" x 8½" rectangle. Press.

4 Repeat step 3 to make a total of 17 rectangles.

5 Using the butterfly blocks, the rain print squares and the pieced rectangles, stitch together the quilt center, referring to the Quilt Layout on the next page for placement. Press.

6 Center and stitch the 3½" x 44½" pink geometric strips to the sides of the quilt center. Press.

7 Stitch the tan print squares to the ends of the 3½" x 32½" pink geometric strips. Press.

8 Stitch the step 7 strips to the top and bottom of the quilt center. Press.

Finish the Quilt

1 Review the instructions for Marking the Quilt Top on page 11 and mark the quilting lines on the quilt top with the marking pen.

2 With the wrong side up, place the backing fabric on the work surface. Carefully smooth out any folds and center the batting on the top of the backing fabric.

3 With the right side up, center the quilt top on the batting.

4 Baste through all layers with pins or with long basting stitches, referring back to the Pinning and Basting section on page 11 for assistance, if necessary.

5 Review the Machine Quilting instructions on page 11 and machine quilt as desired.

6 Remove pins or basting stitches.

7 Trim the thread ends and then trim the edge of the quilt.

8 Stitch the bias binding around the edge of the quilt, as detailed in the Binding instructions on page 11.

The back of the quilt shows the detail of the machine quilting used for this particular design.

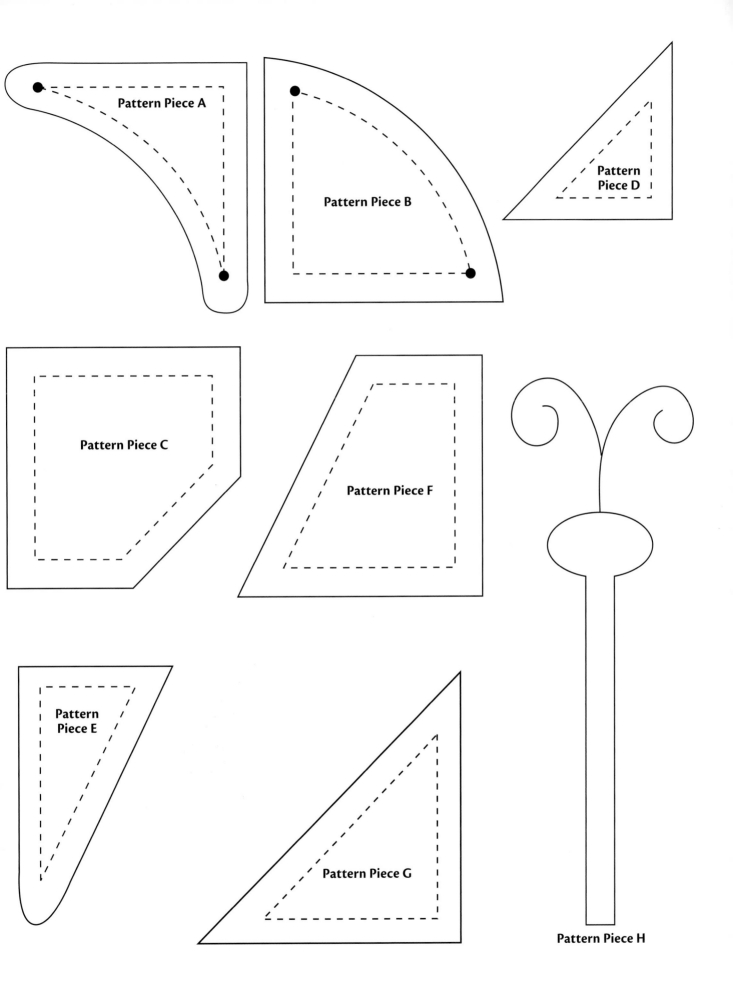

Pattern Piece A

Pattern Piece B

Pattern Piece D

Pattern Piece C

Pattern Piece F

Pattern Piece E

Pattern Piece G

Pattern Piece H

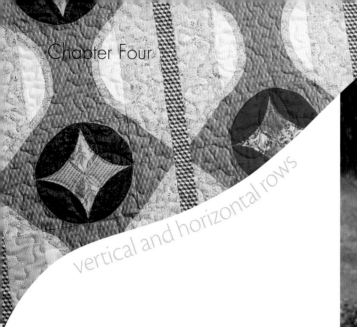

vertical and horizontal rows

Made-to-Order Borders

Both vertical and
horizontal rows are
represented in this chapter.
If you are adventurous, you
can rearrange the blocks to
make concentric borders
or diagonal rows.

Spumoni Row

Spumoni Row

Vanilla, strawberry and pistachio are all displayed in this mélange that serves as an interesting study in color. Compare the differences in the horizontal strips, when the colors change but the patterns stay the same.

Materials Needed

- ¾-yard blue print (strawberry squares, vanilla squares and pistachio squares)
- ⅓-yard cream toile (strawberry squares)
- ¼-yard red print (strawberry squares)
- 1½ yards tan paisley (strawberry squares and border)
- ⅞-yard pink mottle (strawberry squares and pistachio squares)
- ⅓-yard pale peach (vanilla squares)
- ¼-yard cream mini floral (vanilla squares)
- ¼-yard tan script (vanilla squares)
- ½-yard ivory floral (vanilla squares)
- ¼-yard red floral (pistachio squares)
- ¼-yard peach print (pistachio squares)
- ½-yard mint floral (pistachio squares)
- ¼-yard tan marble (horizontal sashing)
- ⅛-yard ivory (horizontal sashing)
- 1¾ yards turquoise print (border)
- 47" x 57" rectangle cotton fabric (backing)
- 47" x 57" rectangle cotton quilt batting
- 5¾ yards 2½"-wide bias binding or prepackaged double-fold bias binding
- Coordinating thread
- 1 sheet 8½" x 11" tracing paper
- 1 sheet 8½" x 11" cardstock
- Air-soluble marking pen

Finished size: 45½" x 55½"
The quilt top measures 46" x 56" before quilting.
    The project will shrink slightly depending on the amount of quilting.
Seam allowances: ¼"
Templates: Use the templates on page 75. Cut on the solid line and stitch on the broken line.

Cutting Plan

From the blue print, cut:
- 30 "A" shapes

From the cream toile, cut:
- 40 "B" shapes

From the red print, cut:
- 40 1⅜" x 3" strips

From the tan paisley, cut:
- 40 1⅜" x 3" strips
- two 2" x 38½" strips
- two 2" x 45½" strips

From the pink mottle, cut:
- 40 "B" shapes
- 40 "C" shapes

From the pale peach, cut:
- 40 "B" shapes

From the cream mini floral, cut:
- 40 1⅜" x 3" strips

From the tan script, cut:
- 40 1⅜" x 3" strips

From the ivory floral, cut:
- 40 "C" shapes

From the red floral, cut:
- 40 1⅜" x 3" strips

From the peach print, cut:
- 40 1⅜" x 3" strips

From the mint floral, cut:
- 40 "C" shapes

From the tan marble, cut:
- eight 2" x 6" strips
- four 2" x 3¼" strips

From the ivory, cut:
- 10 2" squares.

From the turquoise print, cut:
- two 4¼" x 45½" strips
- two 4¼" x 48½" strips

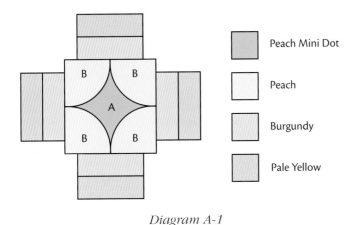

▨	Peach Mini Dot
☐	Peach
▨	Burgundy
▨	Pale Yellow

Diagram A-1

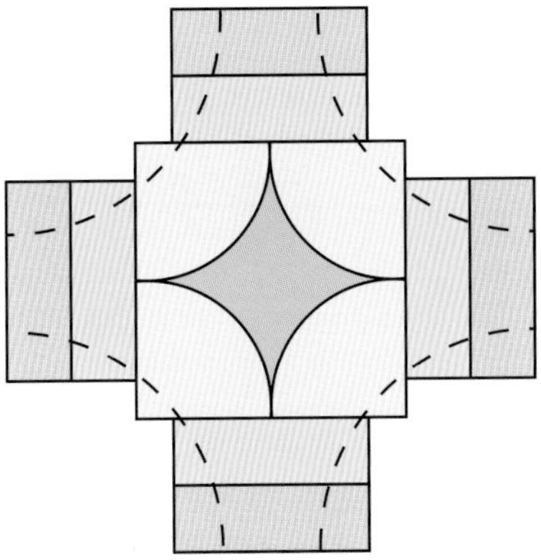

Diagram A-2

Make the Quilt Blocks

1. Match the curved shapes at the dots and stitch four cream toile "B" shapes to one blue print "A" shape, as shown in Diagram A-1 and its accompanying color code. Review the instructions for Curved Patch Piecing on page 9 for assistance, if necessary. Press.

2. Center and stitch four 1⅜" x 3" red print strips and four 1⅜" x 3" tan paisley strips to the "B" shapes. Press.

3. Mark the wrong side of the pieced section, as in Diagram A-2, using the trimmed "C" template. **Note:** Before marking the fabric, the template should be trimmed to the seam line, which is ¼" in from the cutting line and indicated by a broken line on the template.

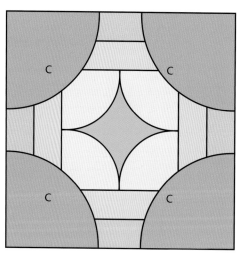

Diagram A-3

Blue Print

Pale Peach

Cream Mini Floral

Tan Script

Ivory Floral

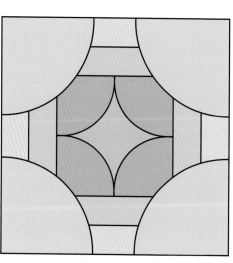

Diagram B-1

Blue Print

Pink Mottle

Red Floral

Peach Print

Mint Floral

Diagram C-1

4 Trim the excess fabric to within ¼" of the marked line and cut perpendicular notches in the seam allowance.

5 Stitch four pink mottle "C" shapes to the trimmed corners of the pieced section to make a square, as shown in Diagram A-3. Press.

6 Repeat steps 1 through 5 nine more times to make a total of 10 squares.

7 Repeat steps 1 through 6, as shown in Diagram B-1 and its color code, but this time substitute four pale peach "B" shapes for the cream toile, four 1⅜" x 3" cream mini floral strips for the red strips, four 1⅜" x 3" tan script strips for the tan paisley strips and four ivory floral "C" shapes for the pink mottle.

8 Repeat steps 1 through 6, as shown in Diagram C-1 and its color code, but this time substitute four pink mottle "B" shapes for the cream toile, four 1⅜" x 3" red floral strips for the red strips, four 1⅜" x 3" peach print strips for the tan paisley strips and four mint floral "C" shapes for the pink mottle.

Assemble the Quilt Top

1 Stitch together the pieced squares into horizontal rows. Alternating each, stitch five 2" ivory squares to the short sides of four 2" x 3¼" tan marble strips. Then stitch 2" x 6" tan marble strips to the ends of the pieced strip. Press. Repeat this step for a second strip.

2 Stitch the pieced strips together to complete the quilt center, referring to the Quilt Layout on the next page for placement.

3 Stitch the 2" x 45½" tan paisley strips to the sides of the quilt center. Press.

4 Stitch the 2" x 38½" tan paisley strips to the top and the bottom of the quilt center. Press.

5 Stitch the 4¼" x 48½" turquoise print strips to the sides of the quilt center. Press.

6 Stitch the 4¼" x 45½" turquoise strips to the top and the bottom of the quilt center. Press.

Quilt Layout

The back of the quilt shows the detail of the machine quilting used for this particular design.

Finish the Quilt

1 Review the instructions for Marking the Quilt Top on page 11 and mark the quilting lines on the quilt top with the marking pen.

2 With the wrong side up, place the backing fabric on the work surface. Carefully smooth out any folds and center the batting on the top of the backing fabric.

3 With the right side up, center the quilt top on the batting.

4 Baste through all layers with pins or with long basting stitches, referring back to the Pinning and Basting section on page 11 for assistance, if necessary.

5 Review the Machine Quilting instructions on page 11 and machine quilt as desired.

6 Remove pins or basting stitches.

7 Trim the thread ends and then trim the edge of the quilt.

8 Stitch the bias binding around the edge of the quilt, as detailed in the Binding instructions on page 11.

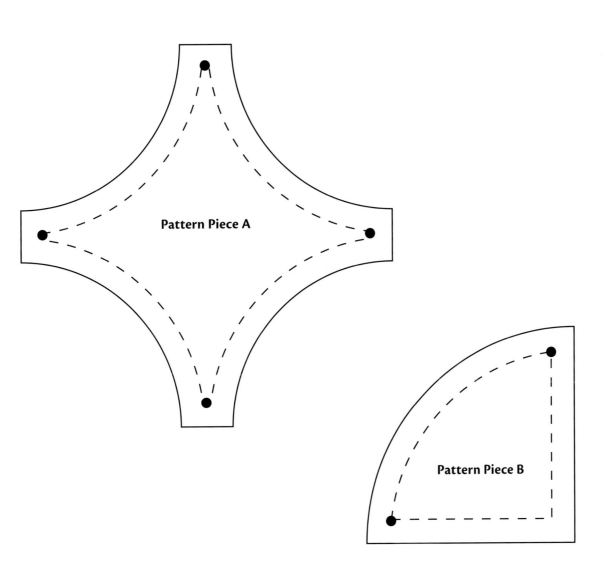

Pattern Piece A

Pattern Piece B

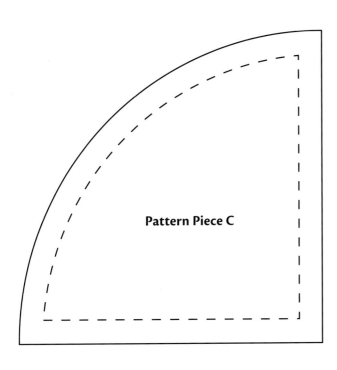

Pattern Piece C

Bands of Gold

Square building blocks combine to form bold vertical
rows that are almost architectural in appearance. The gold
outlines describe the tracery of the curves.

Materials Needed

- ¼-yard gold paisley (circles)
- ¼-yard gold grid (circles)
- ⅛-yard brown floral (circles)
- ⅛-yard pink print (circles)
- ½-yard purple print (circles)
- ¼-yard burgundy (circles)
- 1½ yards gold-on-green print (scallop bands)
- 1 yard gold floral (scallop bands)
- ¾-yard pale yellow (band background)
- 1¼ yards lavender print (band background)
- ¼-yard tan print (band background)
- 1¾ yards wine print (stripes)
- 1¾ yards rose print (border)
- 49" x 61" rectangle cotton fabric (backing)
- 49" x 61" rectangle cotton quilt batting
- 6¼ yards 2½"-wide bias binding or prepackaged double-fold bias binding
- Coordinating thread
- 2 sheets 8½" x 11" tracing paper
- 2 sheets 8½" x 11" cardstock
- Air-soluble marking pen

Finished size: 47" x 59"

The quilt top measures 48" x 60" before quilting. The project will shrink slightly depending on the amount of quilting.

Seam allowances: ¼"

Templates: Use the templates on pages 81 through 83. Cut on the solid line and stitch on the broken line.

Cutting Plan

From the gold paisley, cut:
- 16 2¾" squares

From the gold grid, cut:
- 16 2¾" squares

From the brown floral, cut:
- eight 2¾" squares

From the pink print, cut:
- eight 2¾" squares

From the purple print, cut:
- 32 "A" shapes

From the burgundy, cut:
- 16 "A" shapes

From the gold-on-green print, cut:
- 48 "B" shapes
- 15 "C" shapes
- 32 "D" triangles

From the gold floral, cut:
- 30 "E" shapes
- 64 1" x 6" strips

From the pale yellow, cut:
- 30 "F" shapes

From the lavender print, cut:
- 16 6½" squares
- 32 "G" triangles

From the wine print, cut:
- four 1½" x 54½" strips

From the rose floral, cut:
- two 3¼" x 48" strips
- two 3¼" x 54½" strips

From the tan print, cut:
- four 6½" squares

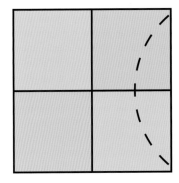

Diagram A-1

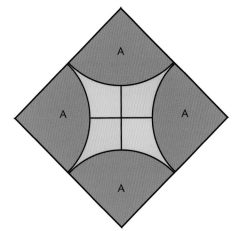

Diagram A-2

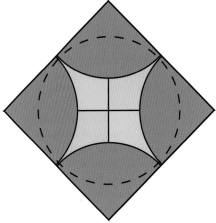

Diagram A-3

Make the Quilt Blocks

1 Alternating colors, stitch two gold paisley squares to two gold grid squares to make a 5" square. Press. Repeat this step to make a total of eight squares.

2 Alternating colors, stitch two brown floral squares to two pink print squares. Press. Repeat this step to make a total of four squares.

3 Mark the wrong side of each of the pieced squares, as in Diagram A-1, using the trimmed "A" template. Note:

Before marking the fabric, the template should be trimmed to the seam line, which is ¼" in from the cutting line and indicated by a broken line.

4 Trim the excess fabric to within ¼" of the marked line and cut perpendicular notches in the seam allowance. Repeat for the remaining sides of each square.

5 Match the curved shapes at the dots and stitch the purple print "A" shapes to the gold paisley-gold

grid trimmed squares, as shown in Diagram A-2. Review the instructions for Curved Patch Piecing on page 9 for assistance, if necessary. Press.

6 Stitch the burgundy "A" shapes to the brown floral-pink print trimmed squares. Press.

7 On the right side of each pieced square, center and mark a 6" circle, as shown in Diagram A-3.

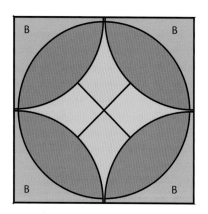

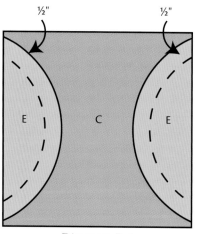

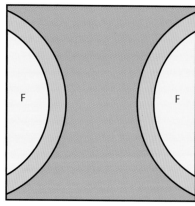

Diagram A-4: "A" Block
("B" Block looks the same, except
with burgundy, brown and pink.)

Diagram B-1

Diagram B-2: "C" Block

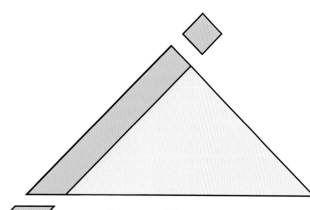

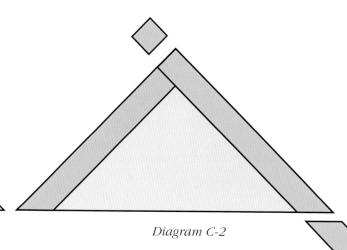

Diagram C-1

Diagram C-2

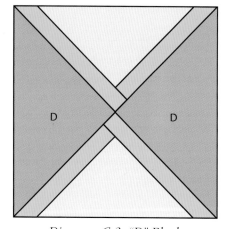

Diagram C-3: "D" Block

8 Trim the excess fabric on each pieced square to within ¼" of the marked line.

9 Rotate each trimmed square and stitch four gold-on-green "B" shapes to the corners to make eight new squares (from four original purple-gold and four original burgundy-brown-pink), as in

Diagram A-4. These are the "A" blocks and "B" blocks. Press.

10 Stitch one gold floral "E" shape to each curved side of the gold-on-green "C" shapes. Press. Repeat for a total of 15 squares.

11 Center and mark the wrong side of the pieced "CE" squares, as in Diagram B-1, using the trimmed "F" template. **Note:** Before marking the fabric, the template should be trimmed to the seam line, which is ¼" in from the cutting line and indicated by a broken line.

12 Trim the excess fabric to within ¼" of the marked line and cut perpendicular notches in the seam allowance for each "CE" square.

13 Stitch the pale yellow "F" shapes to each of the trimmed "CE" squares, as in Diagram B-2. These are the "C" blocks.

14 With the long side of a "G" triangle at the bottom, stitch a gold floral strip to the left side and trim the ends, as in Diagram C-1. Press.

15 Stitch a second strip to the right side of the triangle and trim the ends, as in Diagram C-2. Press.

16 Repeat steps 14 and 15 with the remaining triangles.

17 Stitch two pieced triangles to two "D" triangles, alternating each as in Diagram C-3, to make a "D" block. Repeat to make a total of 16 blocks.

Assemble the Quilt Top

1. Stitch four pieced "D" blocks together with five 6½" lavender print squares, alternating each to make a vertical row, as shown in Diagram D-1. Press.

2. Repeat step 1 to make another vertical row of "D" blocks and lavender print squares, not connected to the first.

3. Repeat step 1, except this time substitute two 6½" tan print squares at the ends of the vertical row.

4. Repeat step 3, making one more vertical row with a tan square at each end. Press.

5. On the wrong side of each vertical strip, center and mark two vertical lines 1" apart.

6. Trim the center fabric from between the lines to within ¼" of each marked line.

7. Stitch the wine print strips to the centers of the vertical rows, as in Diagram D-2. Press.

8. Stitch together two separate vertical rows, alternating five "C" blocks with four "A" blocks, as shown in Diagram E-1. Press.

9. Stitch together one vertical row as in step 8, but this time substituting four "B" blocks for the "A" blocks, as shown in Diagram F-1.

10. Stitch together the vertical rows, referring to the Quilt Layout on the next page for placement. Press.

11. Stitch the 3¼" x 54½" rose floral strips to the sides of the quilt center. Press.

12. Stitch the 3¼" x 48" rose floral strips to the top and the bottom of the quilt center. Press.

Diagram D-1   Diagram D-2   Diagram E-1   Diagram F-1

Quilt Layout

Finish the Quilt

1 Review the instructions for Marking the Quilt Top on page 11 and mark the quilting lines on the quilt top with the marking pen.

2 With the wrong side up, place the backing fabric on the work surface. Carefully smooth out any folds and center the batting on the top of the backing fabric.

3 With the right side up, center the quilt top on the batting.

4 Baste through all layers with pins or with long basting stitches, referring back to the Pinning and Basting section on page 11 for assistance, if necessary.

5 Review the Machine Quilting instructions on page 11 and machine quilt as desired.

6 Remove pins or basting stitches.

7 Trim the thread ends and then trim the edge of the quilt.

8 Stitch the bias binding around the edge of the quilt, as detailed in the Binding instructions on page 11.

The back of the quilt shows the detail of the machine quilting used for this particular design.

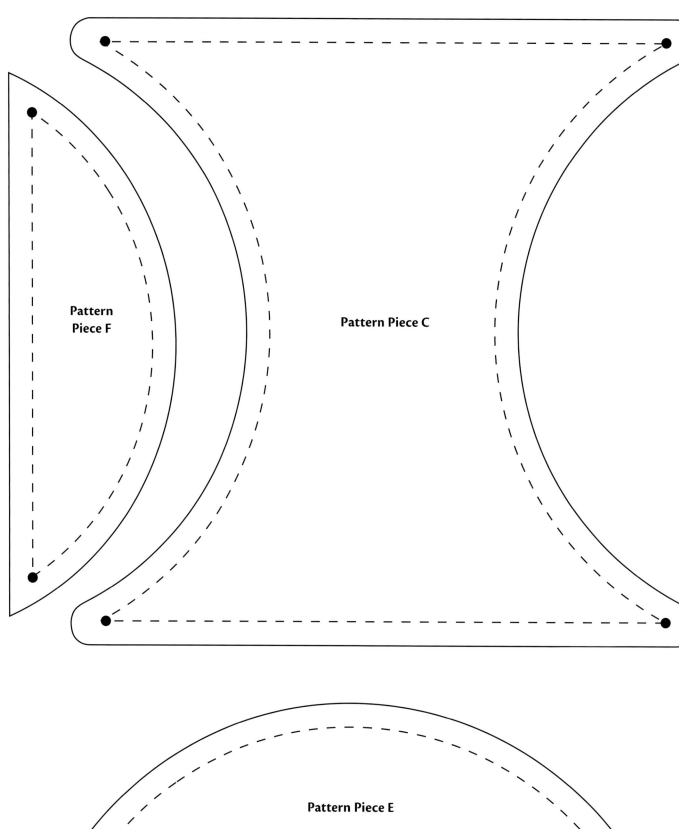

Pattern
Piece F

Pattern Piece C

Pattern Piece E

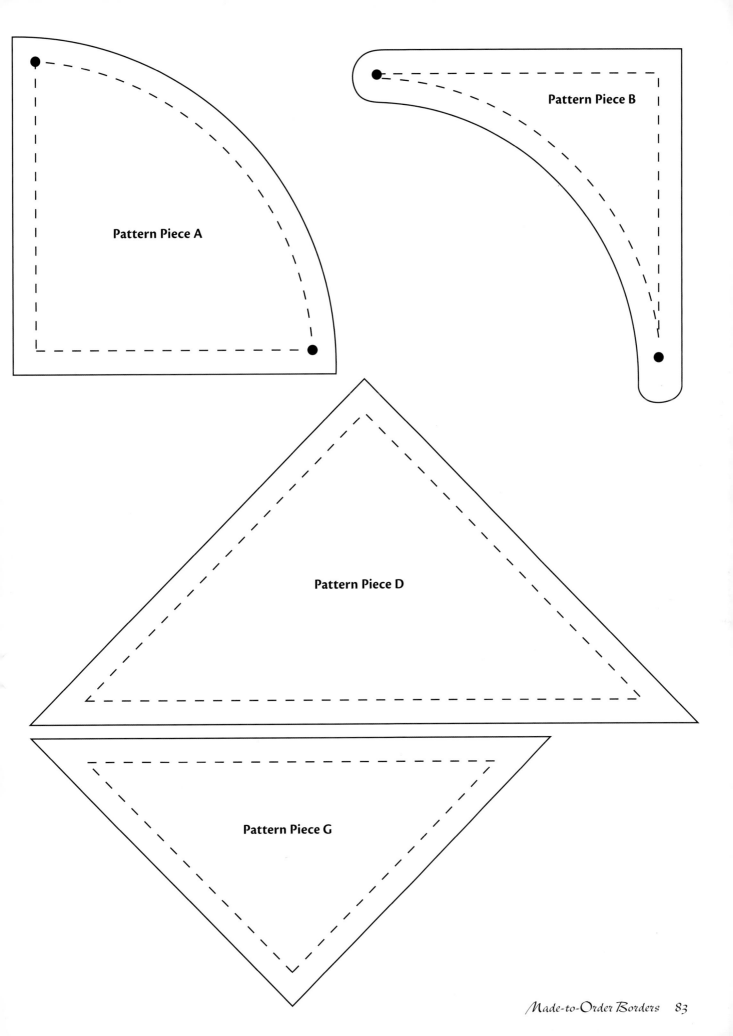

Pattern Piece A

Pattern Piece B

Pattern Piece D

Pattern Piece G

Bows for Baby

These stacked bows make up a quilt that is the perfect fit for a baby crib in a pastel nursery. If you don't have a baby, use it to decorate a wooden chair in a country kitchen.

Materials Needed

- 1¼ yards dark pink floral
  (bows and border)
- ⅛-yard pastel stripe (bows)
- ¼-yard green dot (bows)
- ¼-yard green grid (bows)
- 1 yard ivory print (butterfly background)
- ½-yard blue mini stars print (blue rows)
- ¾-yard light pink floral
  (blue rows and border)
- ⅛-yard blue stripe (border)
- ¼-yard pink mottle (border)
- 45" x 46" rectangle cotton fabric (backing)
- 45" x 46" rectangle cotton quilt batting
- 5 yards 2½"-wide bias binding or
  prepackaged double-fold bias binding
- Coordinating thread
- 2 sheets 8½" x 11" tracing paper
- 2 sheets 8½" x 11" cardstock
- Air-soluble marking pen

Finished size: 43½" x 45"

The quilt top measures 44" x 45½" before quilting.
  The project will shrink slightly depending on the
  amount of quilting.

Seam allowances: ¼"

Templates: Use the templates on pages 88 and 89.
  Cut on the solid line and stitch on the broken line.

Cutting Plan

From the dark pink floral, cut:
- 15 "A" shapes
- 15 reverse "A" shapes
- 30 1½" x 6¾" strips
- four "G" triangles
  (Enlarge the template to the
  specified size before cutting.)

From the pastel stripe, cut:
- 15 2" x 1½" rectangles

From the green dot, cut:
- 14 "B" shapes

From the green grid, cut:
- 16 "B" shapes

From the blue stripe, cut:
- two 1¾" x 34" strips

From the ivory print, cut:
- 15 "C" shapes
- 15 "D" triangles
- 30 1½" x 6" strips

From the blue mini-stars print, cut:
- 20 "E" shapes

From the light pink floral, cut:
- four 4¼" x 36½" strips
  (Cut these long strips first.)
- 40 "F" shapes

From the pink mottle, cut:
- two 1¾" x 34" strips
- two 1¾" x 35½" strips

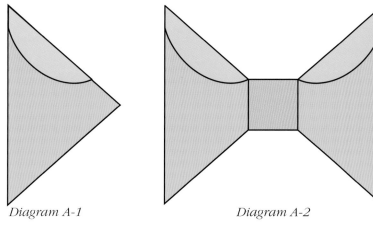

Diagram A-1   *Diagram A-2*

Diagram A-2

Make the Quilt Blocks

1 Match the curved shapes at the dots
  and stitch a dark pink "A" shape
and the dark pink reverse "A" shapes to
the green dot "B" shapes, as shown in
Diagram A-1. Review the instructions
for Curved Patch Piecing on page 9 for
assistance, if necessary. Press.

2 Stitch one pair of "AB" shapes to one
  2" x 1½" pastel stripe rectangle, as in
Diagram A-2, to make a bow.

3 Review the instructions for Insetting
  Diagonal Pieces on page 9 and match
the diagonal side of one ivory print "C"
shape to the top of a pieced bow, as in
Diagram A-3.

4 Stitch together the "C" shape to the
  pieced bow, starting and stopping ¼"
from each edge.

5 Realign the raw edges and stitch the
  remaining two sides of the "C" shape
to the bow. Press.

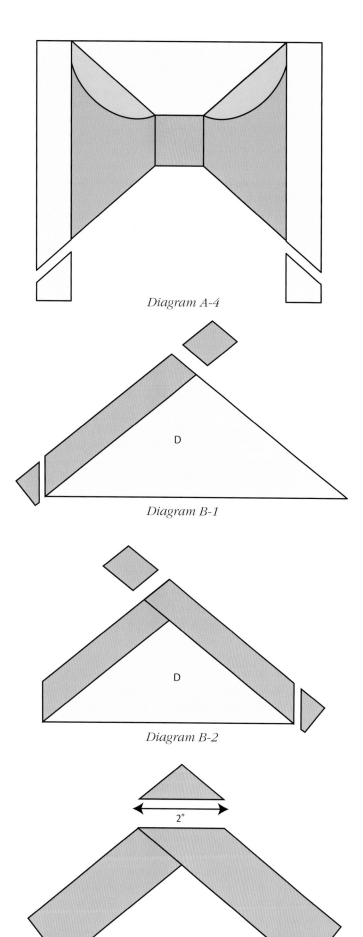

Diagram A-4

Diagram B-1

Diagram B-2

2"

Diagram B-3

6 Matching top edges, stitch a 1½" x 6" ivory strip to each side of the pieced bow. Press.

7 Trim the ends of the strips at the same angle as the bow bottom, as in Diagram A-4.

8 With the long side of an ivory print "D" triangle at the bottom, stitch a 1½" x 6¾" dark pink floral strip to the left side and trim the ends, as shown in Diagram B-1. Press.

9 Stitch a second 1½" x 6¾" dark pink floral strip to the right side of the triangle and trim the ends, as in Diagram B-2.

10 Trim the top of the triangle, as shown in Diagram B-3.

11 Stitch the pieced triangle to the bottom of the bow. Press.

12 Repeat steps 1 through 11, substituting the green grid "B" shapes when all the green dot "B" shapes are used up, to make a total of 15 bow blocks.

13 Match the curved shapes at the dots and stitch two light pink floral "F" shapes to one blue mini-stars "E" shape. Press.

14 Repeat step 13 to make a total of 20 "EF" rectangles.

Assemble the Quilt Top

1 Stitch the bow blocks and "EF" rectangles together in vertical rows, referring to the Quilt Layout on the next page for placement. Press.

2 Stitch the 1¾" x 34" blue stripe strips to the top and the bottom of the quilt center. Press.

3 Stitch the 1¾" x 34" pink mottle strips to the top and the bottom of the quilt center. Press.

4 Center and stitch the 1¾" x 35½" pink mottle strips to the sides of the quilt center. Press.

5 Center and stitch two 4¼" x 36½" light pink floral strips to the top and the bottom of the quilt center. Press.

6 Center and stitch the remaining two 4¼" x 36½" light pink floral strips to the sides of the quilt center. Press.

7 Mark a diagonal line on the wrong side of the quilt top at each corner, as shown in Diagram C-1.

8 Trim excess fabric to within ¼" of the marked lines.

9 Match the long sides of the dark pink floral "G" triangles to the marked lines and stitch together to make the corners of the quilt top, again referring to the Quilt Layout for assistance. Press.

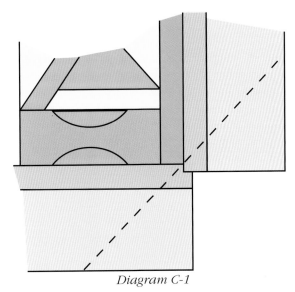

Diagram C-1

Quilt Layout

Finish the Quilt

1 Review the instructions for Marking the Quilt Top on page 11 and mark the quilting lines on the quilt top with the marking pen.

2 With the wrong side up, place the backing fabric on the work surface. Carefully smooth out any folds and center the batting on the top of the backing fabric.

3 With the right side up, center the quilt top on the batting.

4 Baste through all layers with pins or with long basting stitches, referring back to the Pinning and Basting section on page 11 for assistance, if necessary.

5 Review the Machine Quilting instructions on page 11 and machine quilt as desired.

6 Remove pins or basting stitches.

7 Trim the thread ends and then trim the edge of the quilt.

8 Stitch the bias binding around the edge of the quilt, as detailed in the Binding instructions on page 11.

The back of the quilt shows the detail of the machine quilting used for this particular design.

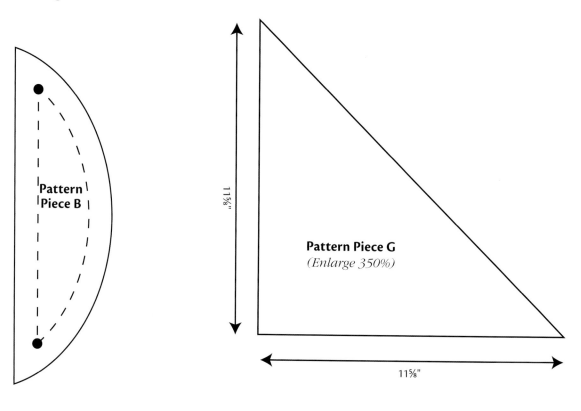

Pattern Piece B

11⅝"

Pattern Piece G
(Enlarge 350%)

11⅝"

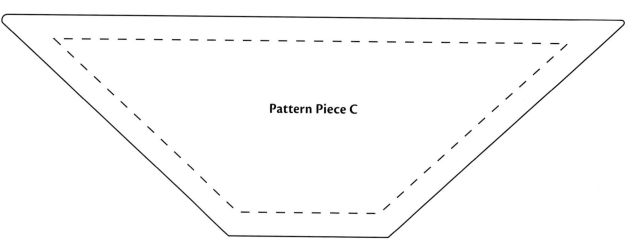

Pattern Piece C

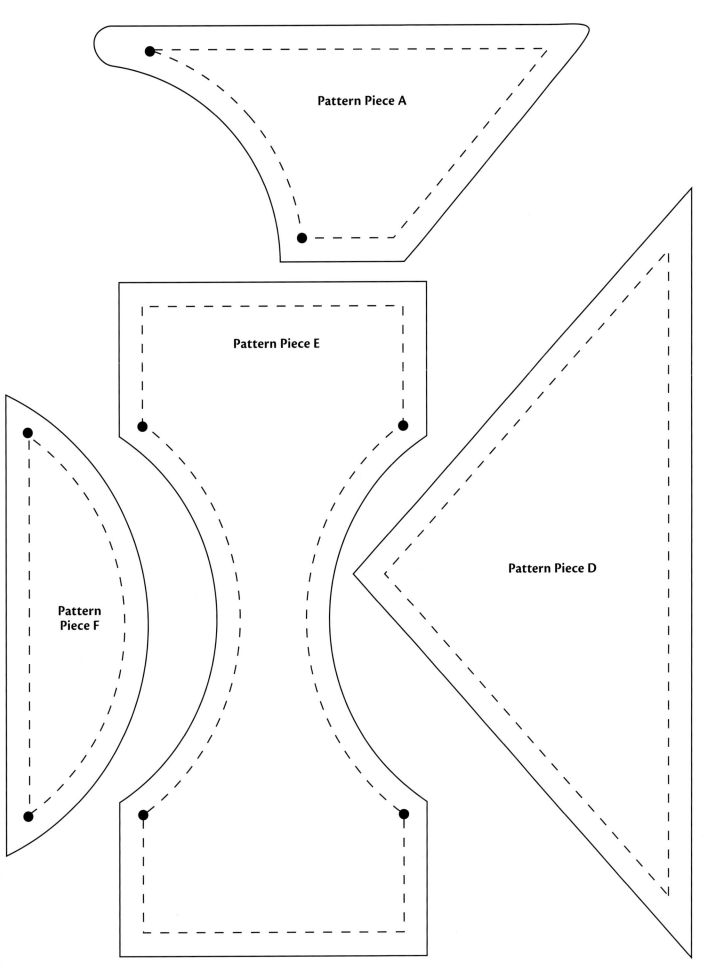

Pattern Piece A

Pattern Piece E

Pattern Piece F

Pattern Piece D

favorite times of the year

Four Seasons

Any quilter can tell you that the subject and tone of a project is influenced by the ambience, including the season of the year and the feel in the air. Pick your favorite times of the year and rejoice in them with these seasonal quilts.

Here Comes the Sun

Usher in the spring with a quilt that is an
explosion of color and energy.

Materials Needed

- 1 yard gold print (sun blocks)
- ¼-yard each of six to eight yellow solids and yellow prints (sun blocks)
- ¼ yard orange mottle (sun blocks)
- 1¼ yards medium blue (sun blocks and flower blocks)
- 1 yard blue print (sun blocks)
- 1 yard light blue (flower blocks)
- 1 yard ivory (flower blocks)
- ½-yard olive print (flower blocks)
- ¼-yard salmon print (flower blocks)
- 1¼ yards light pink print (pink squares)
- 1¼ yards dark pink print (pink squares)
- 53" square cotton fabric (backing)
- 53" square cotton quilt batting
- 6 yards 2½"-wide bias binding or prepackaged double-fold bias binding
- ½-yard lightweight tear-away stabilizer for machine embroidery
- 1 skein green embroidery floss
- Salmon thread
- Olive thread
- Coordinating thread
- 2 sheets 8½" x 11" tracing paper
- 2 sheets 8½" x 11" cardstock
- Air-soluble marking pen

Finished size: 52" square

The quilt measures 52½" square before quilting. The project will shrink slightly depending upon the amount of quilting.

Seam allowances: ¼"

Templates: Use the templates on pages 99 and 100. Cut on the solid line and stitch on the broken line.

Cutting Plan

From the gold print, cut:
- 36 "E" shapes
- 72 "C" triangles
- 12 6" lengths, each one between 1" to 3" wide

From the yellow solids and prints, cut:
- 24 6" lengths, each one between 1" to 3" wide

From the orange mottle, cut:
- 36 "C" triangles

From the medium blue, cut:
- 36 "B" shapes
- 36 "C" triangles
- four 11" squares
- 48 2½" squares

From the blue print, cut:
- 36 "D" shapes
- 72 "F" triangles

From the light blue, cut:
- 12 4" squares
- 48 1" x 2½" strips
- 48 1" x 3" strips
- 96 1½" x 3" strips

From the ivory, cut:
- 48 "H" shapes
- 48 reverse "H" shapes
- 48 "G" triangles

From the olive print, cut:
- 48 "I" leaves

From the salmon print, cut:
- 48 1¾" circles

From the light pink print, cut:
- 52 "G" triangles

From the dark pink print, cut:
- 48 "G" triangles

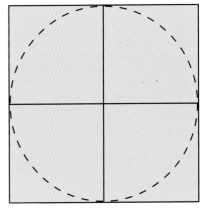

Diagram A-1

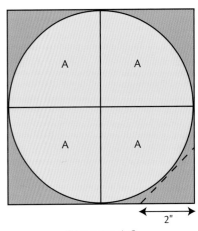

Diagram A-2

Make the Quilt Blocks
Sun Blocks

1 Stitch the 6" lengths of gold print, yellow solids and yellow prints together to make 36 6" squares. Stitch in random order and angle the strips slightly, if desired. Press.

2 From each pieced 6" square, cut an "A" shape (36 total).

3 Stitch the straight sides of four "A" shapes together to make a circle. Repeat for a total of nine circles. Press.

4 Make a 6½"-wide circle template.

5 Mark the right sides of the pieced "A" circles, using the circle template and the marking pen.

6 Match the curved shapes at the dots and stitch four "B" shapes to each

circle to make nine squares, as shown in Diagram A-1. Review the instructions for Curved Patch Piecing on page 9 for assistance, if necessary. Press.

7 Use the marking pen to mark a diagonal line on the wrong side of the one square at each corner, as in Diagram A-2.

8 Trim excess fabric to within ¼" of the marked line.

9 Stitch the long sides of four orange "C" triangles to the marked lines to make a square. Press.

10 Repeat steps 7 through 9 to make a total of nine "sun centers" and set aside.

11 Stitch the gold print "E" shapes to the blue print "D" shapes. Press.

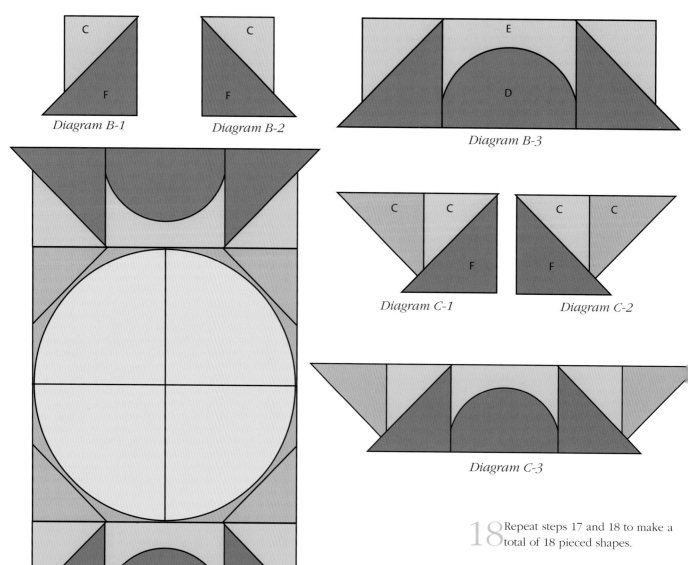

Diagram B-1

Diagram B-2

Diagram B-3

Diagram C-1

Diagram C-2

Diagram C-3

Diagram B-4

12 Match the top corners and stitch the long side of one gold "C" triangle to the long side of one blue print "F" triangle, as in Diagram B-1. Press. Repeat this step to make a total of 18 pieced sections.

13 Match the top corners and stitch the long side of one gold "C" triangle to the long side of one "F" triangle, as Diagram B-2, to create a mirror image to the pieced section from step 12. Press. Repeat this step to make a total of 18 pieced sections.

14 Stitch one pair of pieced "CF" triangles to one "DE" pieced rectangle, as shown in Diagram B-3.

Press. Repeat to make a total of 18 pieced sections.

15 Stitch the "CF-DE" pieced sections to the top and the bottom of a sun center, as shown in Diagram B-4. Press. Repeat this step with the remaining eight sun centers.

16 Stitch the short side of one gold print "C" triangle to the short side of one medium blue "C" triangle (gold on the left, blue on the right).

17 Match the top corners and stitch the long side of the blue "C" triangle to the long side of a blue print "F" triangle, as shown in Diagram C-1.

18 Repeat steps 17 and 18 to make a total of 18 pieced shapes.

19 Stitch the short side of a gold print "C" triangle to the short side of a medium blue "C" triangle (blue on the right, gold on the left).

20 Match the top corners and stitch the long side of the gold "C" triangle to the long side of a blue print "F" triangle, as in Diagram C-2.

21 Repeat steps 19 and 20 to make a total of 18 pieced shapes.

22 Stitch one pair of pieced "CF" triangles to one "DE" rectangle, as in Diagram C-3. Press. Repeat this step to make a total of 18 pieced sections.

23 Stitch the pieced sections to the sides of the sun centers. Press.

24 Use the marking pen on the wrong side of each of the sun centers to mark a diagonal line at each corner, as in Diagram D-1.

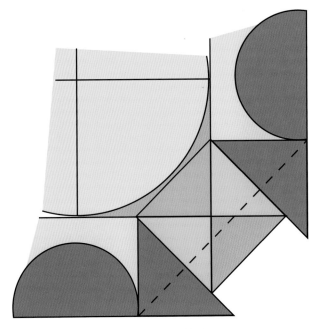

Diagram D-1

Diagram E-1: Sun Block

25 Trim excess fabric to within ¼" of the marked lines.

26 Stitch the long sides of four light pink print "G" triangles to the marked lines to make a square, as shown in Diagram E-1. Press. Repeat this step to make a total of nine sun blocks.

Flower Blocks

1 Center and baste one salmon circle (flower) to one 2½" medium blue square. Review the Pinning and Basting instruction on page 11, if necessary.

2 Cut one 2½" square of interfacing and layer it on the wrong side of the blue square.

3 On a scrap of fabric, machine satin stitch a short straight line. Adjust your machine to the desired line width and coverage. The width of the stitching line on the photo model is ⅛".

4 With the salmon thread, satin stitch around the circle flower.

5 Trim the thread ends and remove the basting stitches.

6 Carefully tear the stabilizer from the inside and the outside of the flower.

7 Repeat steps 1 through 6 to make a total of 48 flowers.

8 Mark the center of each circle flower with air-soluble pen.

9 Use three strands of the embroidery floss and stitch a French knot on each circle flower. Review the Hand-Embroidery on page 10 for assistance, if necessary.

10 Stitch one light blue 1" x 2½" strip and one light blue 1" x 3" strip to a flower square, as shown in Diagram F-1. Press.

11 Stitch two light blue 1½" x 3¼" strips to the remaining sides of the square, as in Diagram F-2. Press.

12 Repeat steps 10 and 11 to make a total of 48 pieced sections.

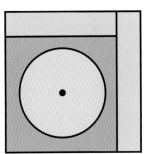

Diagram F-1

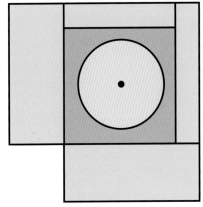

Diagram F-2

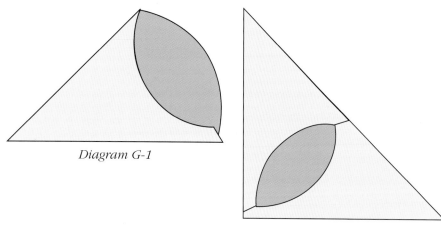

Diagram G-1

Diagram G-2

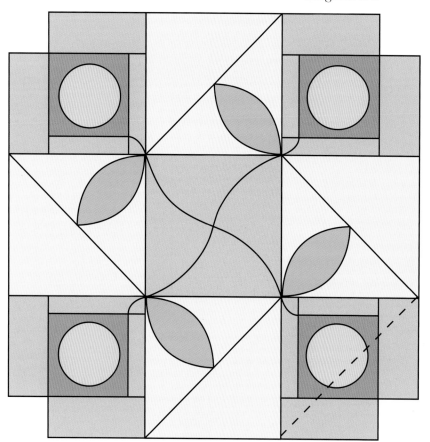

Diagram H-1

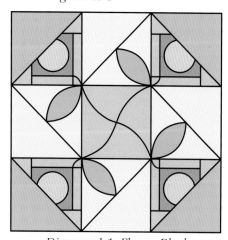

Diagram I-1: Flower Block

13 Stitch one ivory "H" shape to one olive print "I" leaf, as in Diagram G-1.

14 Stitch a reverse "H" shape to the "I" leaf to make a triangle, as shown in Diagram G-2. Press.

15 Stitch the long side of the pieced leaf triangle to the long side of an ivory "G" triangle to make a square. Press.

16 Repeat steps 13 through 15 to make a total of 48 squares.

17 Stitch together one light blue square, four leaf squares and four flower sections, as shown in Diagram H-1.

18 Mark the vines in the center with air-soluble pen.

19 Cut one 6" square of interfacing and center it on the wrong side of the flower block.

20 On a scrap of fabric, machine satin stitch a short straight line. Adjust your machine to the desired line width and coverage. The width of the stitching line on the photo model is ⅛".

21 With the olive thread, satin stitch along the marked lines.

22 Trim the thread ends.

23 Use the marking pen to mark diagonal lines on the wrong side of the block at the corners, referring to Diagram D-1 from step 24 in the Sun Block instructions for assistance, if necessary.

24 Trim the excess fabric to within ¼" of the marked line.

25 Stitch the long sides of four dark pink print "G" triangles to the marked lines to make a finished square, as shown in Diagram I-1. Press.

26 Repeat steps 17 through 25 to make a total of 12 squares.

Blue Blocks

1 Use the marking pen to mark diagonal lines at the corners on the wrong sides of each 11" medium blue square, as in Diagram J-1.

2 Trim excess fabric to within ¼" of the marked lines.

3 Stitch four light pink print triangles to the corners, as in Diagram K-1. Press. Repeat this step to make a total of four blue blocks.

Assemble the Quilt Top

1 Stitch together the sun blocks, the flower blocks and the blue squares, as shown in the Quilt Layout below. Press.

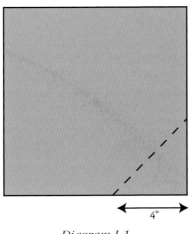

Diagram J-1

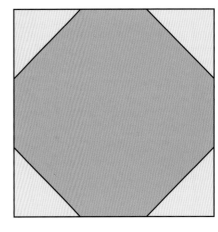

Diagram K-1: Blue Block

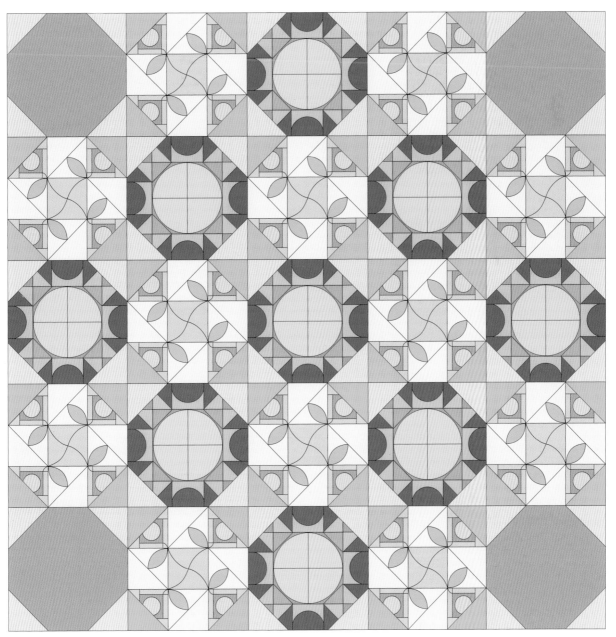

Quilt Layout

Finish the Quilt

1 Review the instructions for Marking the Quilt Top on page 11 and mark the quilting lines on the quilt top with the marking pen.

2 With the wrong side up, place the backing fabric on the work surface. Carefully smooth out any folds and center the batting on the top of the backing fabric.

3 With the right side up, center the quilt top on the batting.

4 Baste through all layers with pins or with long basting stitches, referring back to the Pinning and Basting section on page 11 for assistance, if necessary.

5 Review the Machine Quilting instructions on page 11 and machine quilt as desired.

6 Remove pins or basting stitches.

7 Trim the thread ends and then trim the edge of the quilt.

8 Stitch the bias binding around the edge of the quilt, as detailed in the Binding instructions on page 11.

The back of the quilt shows the detail of the machine quilting used for this particular design.

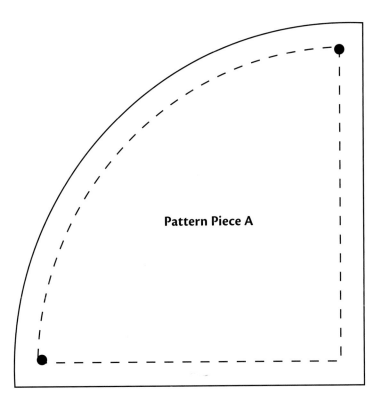

Pattern Piece A

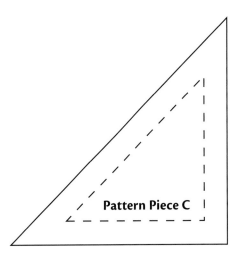

Pattern Piece C

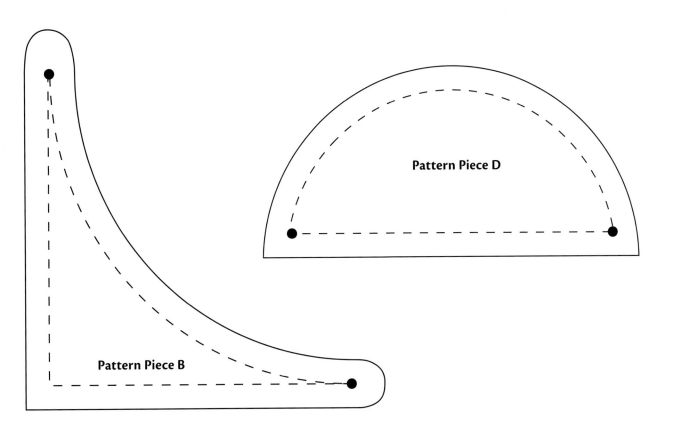

Pattern Piece B

Pattern Piece D

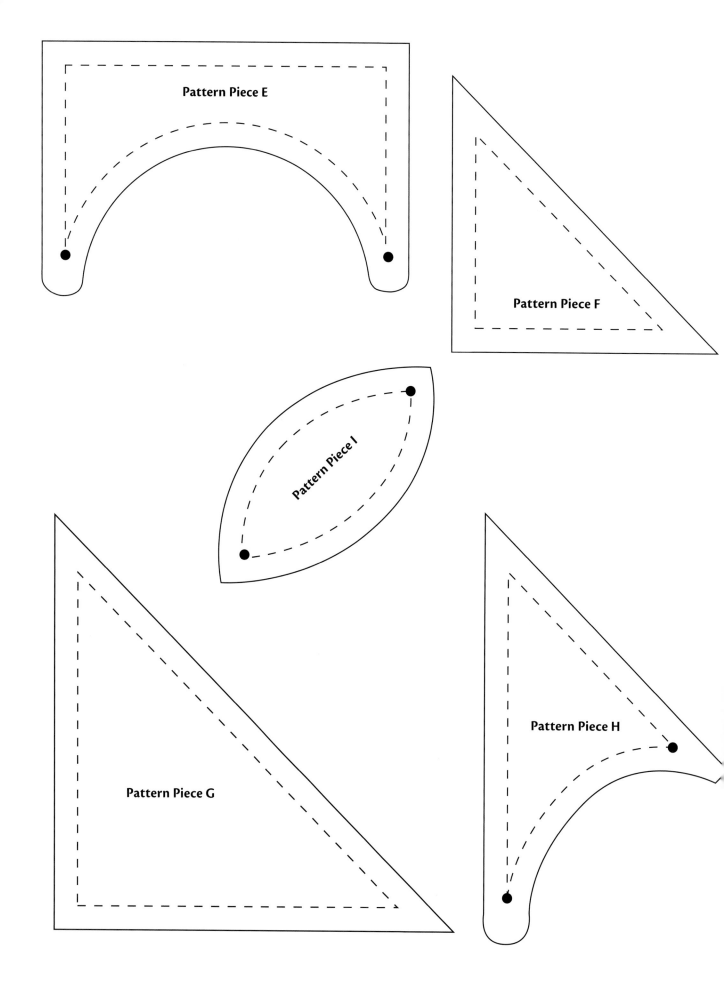

Pattern Piece E

Pattern Piece F

Pattern Piece I

Pattern Piece G

Pattern Piece H

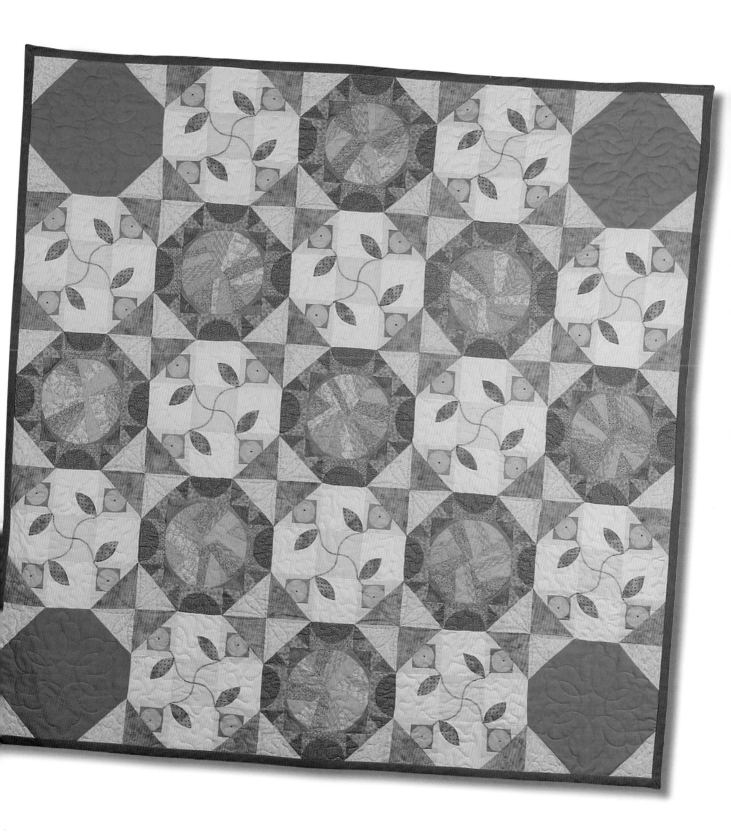

Into the Woods

This quilt depicts a summer at the lake, rendered in fabric and lacking only the mosquitoes. Hand-appliquéd shapes with their organic outlines act as a complement to a uniform row of geometric trees.

Materials Needed

- ¼-yard light blue dot (pieced squares)
- ½-yard dark blue floral (pieced squares)
- 1 yard medium blue wave
  (pieced squares and background)
- ⅓-yard olive (pieced squares and trees)
- ¼-yard light green print (background)
- ½-yard dark green print (trees)
- ½-yard cream print (tree background)
- ⅛-yard light blue wave (stripes)
- ⅛-yard purple (stripes and appliqué)
- ⅛-yard medium green print (stripes)
- ⅛-yard gold (appliqué)
- ¼-yard cream rain print (appliqué)
- ⅛-yard lavender print (appliqué)
- ⅛-yard ivory (appliqué)
- ⅛-yard yellow (appliqué)
- ⅛-yard black print (appliqué)
- ⅛-yard brown print (appliqué)
- ⅛-yard burgundy (appliqué)
- ⅛-yard gray print (appliqué)
- ⅛-yard rust print (appliqué)
- ⅛-yard red print (appliqué)
- 32" x 43" square cotton fabric (backing)
- 32" x 43" square cotton quilt batting
- 4¼ yards 2½" wide bias binding or
  prepackaged double-fold bias binding
- ¼-yard lightweight tear-away stabilizer
  for machine embroidery
- Cream thread
- Black thread
- Coordinating thread
- 5½ sheets 8½" x 11" tracing paper
- 5½ sheets 8½" x 11" cardstock
- Air-soluble marking pen

Finished size: 30" x 41½"
The quilt measures 30½" x 42" before quilting.
  The project will shrink slightly depending upon the
  amount of quilting.
Seam allowances: ¼"
Templates: Use the templates on pages 107 through 112.
  Cut on the solid line and stitch on the broken line.

Cutting Plan

Note: Hand-appliquéd templates do not include a seam allowance. Allow at least ¼" around the shapes when cutting. The clouds and star are machine appliqués and require no seam allowance.

From the light blue dot, cut:
- eight "A" shapes

From the dark blue floral, cut:
- 48 "B" shapes

From the medium blue wave, cut:
- 32 "C" shapes
- eight "D" triangles
- four "E" triangles

From the olive, cut:
- 32 2" squares
- 20 "F" triangles
- 20 reverse "F" triangles

From the light green print, cut:
- five 7½" squares

From the dark green print, cut:
- 15 "F" triangles
- 15 reverse "F" triangles
- 30 "G" shapes

From the cream print, cut:
- 30 "H" shapes
- 10 2½" squares
- five "F" triangles
- five reverse "F" triangles

From the light blue wave, cut:
- one 1½" x 30½" strip

From the purple, cut:
- one 1½" x 30½" strip
- one door

From the medium green print, cut:
- one 2" x 30½" strip

From the gold, cut:
- one star

From the cream rain print, cut:
- two clouds

From the lavender print, cut:
- one chimney

From the ivory, cut:
- one pediment
- one house side

From the yellow, cut:
- one house front

From the black print, cut:
- one large roof
- one small roof

From the brown print, cut:
- three logs

From the burgundy, cut:
- two fish

From the gray print, cut:
- two fin sets

From the rust print, cut:
- one fish

From the red print, cut:
- one fin set

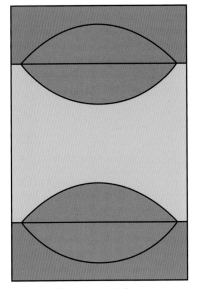

Diagram A-1

Make the Quilt Blocks

1 Match the curved shapes at the dots and stitch one dark blue floral "B" shape to one side of a light blue dot "A" shape and a second dark blue floral "B" shape to the other side of the same "A" shape to make a square. Review the instructions for Curved Patch Piecing on page 9 for assistance, if necessary. Press.

2 Repeat step 1 to make a total of eight squares.

3 Stitch one "B" shape to one "C" shape. Press.

4 Repeat step 3 to make a total of 32 pieced rectangles.

5 Stitch two pieced rectangles to the top and the bottom of one pieced square, as shown in Diagram A-1. Press.

6 Repeat step 5 to make a total of eight pieced sections.

7 Stitch two 2" olive squares to the ends of the remaining pieced rectangles. Press.

8 Stitch the rectangles to the sides of the squares, as shown in Diagram A-2, to complete eight circle blocks.

9 Stitch one pair of olive "F" triangles together to make a large triangle, as in Diagram B-1.

10 Stitch one pair of dark green print "F" triangles to the olive triangle to make a square, as in Diagram B-2. Press.

11 Repeat steps 9 and 10 to make a total of 15 olive-dark green print squares.

12 Repeat steps 9 and 10, but this time substitute the pairs of cream print "F" triangles for the dark green print used before, and make five olive-cream print squares. Press.

13 Match the curved shapes at the dots and stitch together one dark green print "G" shape and one cream print "H" shape to form a square.

14 Repeat step 13 for the remaining "G" and "H" shapes to make a total of 30 "GH" squares.

15 Stitch together one olive-cream print square, three olive-dark green print squares, six "GH" squares and two olive-cream print squares, as shown in Diagram B-3, to make a tree block.

16 Repeat step 15 to make a total of five tree blocks.

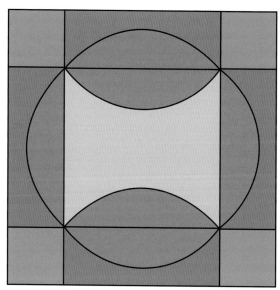

Diagram A-2: Circle Block

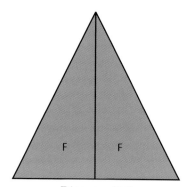

Diagram B-1

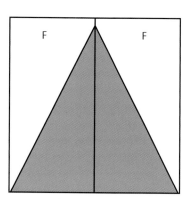

Diagram B-2

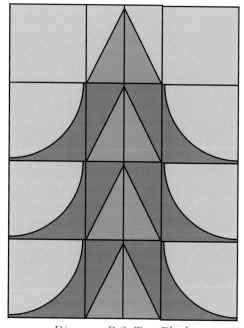

Diagram B-3: Tree Block

Diagram D-1

The back of the quilt shows the detail of the machine quilting used for this particular design.

Assemble the Quilt Top

1 Stitch together the five 7½" green print squares, the eight pieced circle blocks (Diagram A-2), eight medium blue wave "D" triangles and the four medium blue wave "E" triangles, as shown in Diagram D-1. Press.

2 Stitch the long sides of the tree blocks together to form a horizontal row. Press.

3 Stitch together the large pieced square, the trees, the light blue wave strip, the purple strip and the green print strip, as shown in the Quilt Layout on page 106. Press.

4 Pin the left cloud in place, referring to the Quilt Layout on the next page for placement, and with the cream thread, stitch around the edge of the cloud appliqué with a narrow zigzag stitch. Review the Hand-Appliqué instructions on page 10 for assistance, if necessary.

5 Noting overlaps, appliqué the cabin and the fish to the quilt center, again referring to the Quilt Layout for placement.

6 Pin the right cloud and the star in place and with the cream thread, stitch around the edge with a narrow zigzag stitch.

7 With the marking pen and the letter template from page 112, mark the wording or draw your own on the quilt center.

8 Cut a piece of stabilizer slightly larger than the wording.

9 Adjust your machine to the desired line width and coverage. The width of the stitching line on the photo model is ⅛". With the black thread, stitch along the marked lines and trim the thread ends.

Finish the Quilt

1 Review the instructions for Marking the Quilt Top on page 11 and mark the quilting lines on the quilt top with the marking pen.

2 With the wrong side up, place the backing fabric on the work surface. Carefully smooth out any folds and center the batting on the top of the backing fabric.

3 With the right side up, center the quilt top on the batting.

4 Baste through all layers with pins or with long basting stitches, referring back to the Pinning and Basting section on page 11 for assistance, if necessary.

5 Review the Machine Quilting instructions on page 11 and machine quilt as desired.

6 Remove pins or basting stitches.

7 Trim the thread ends and then trim the edge of the quilt.

8 Stitch the bias binding around the edge of the quilt, as detailed in the Binding instructions on page 11.

Quilt Layout

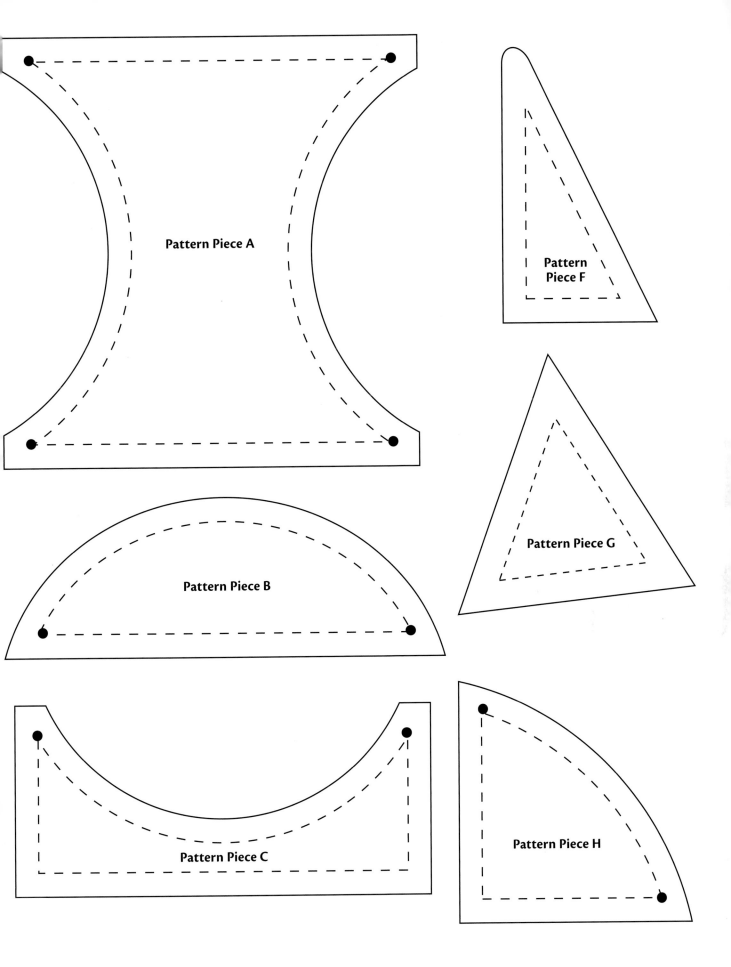

Pattern Piece A

Pattern Piece B

Pattern Piece C

Pattern Piece F

Pattern Piece G

Pattern Piece H

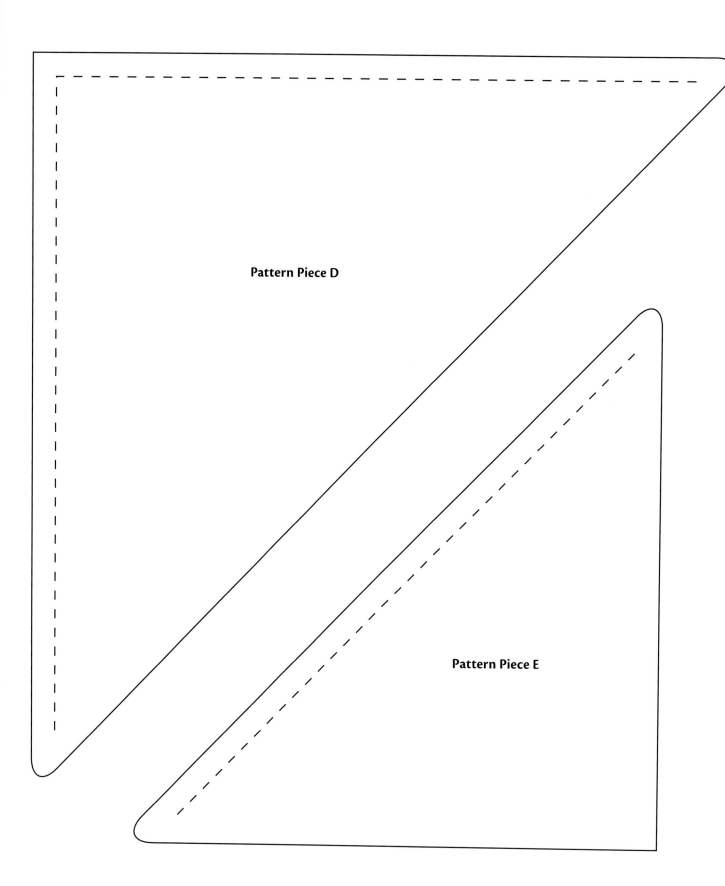

Pattern Piece D

Pattern Piece E

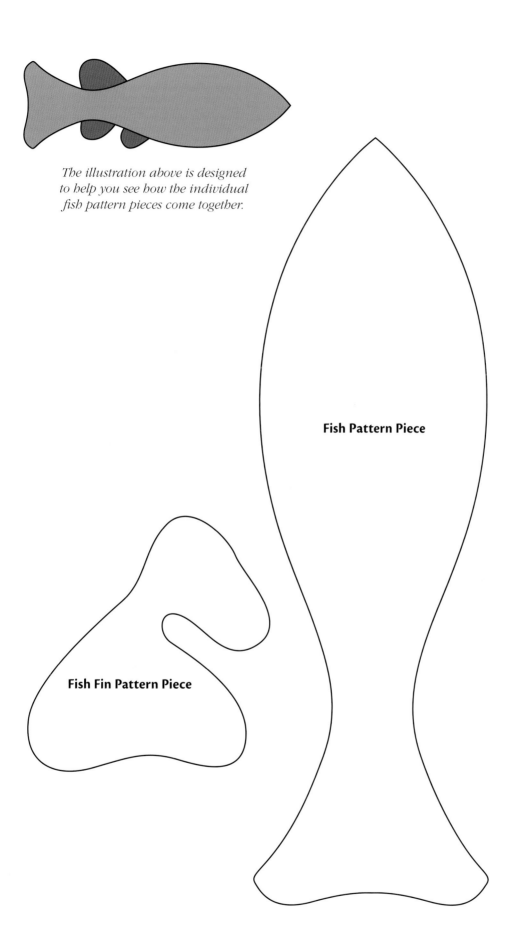

The illustration above is designed to help you see how the individual fish pattern pieces come together.

Fish Pattern Piece

Fish Fin Pattern Piece

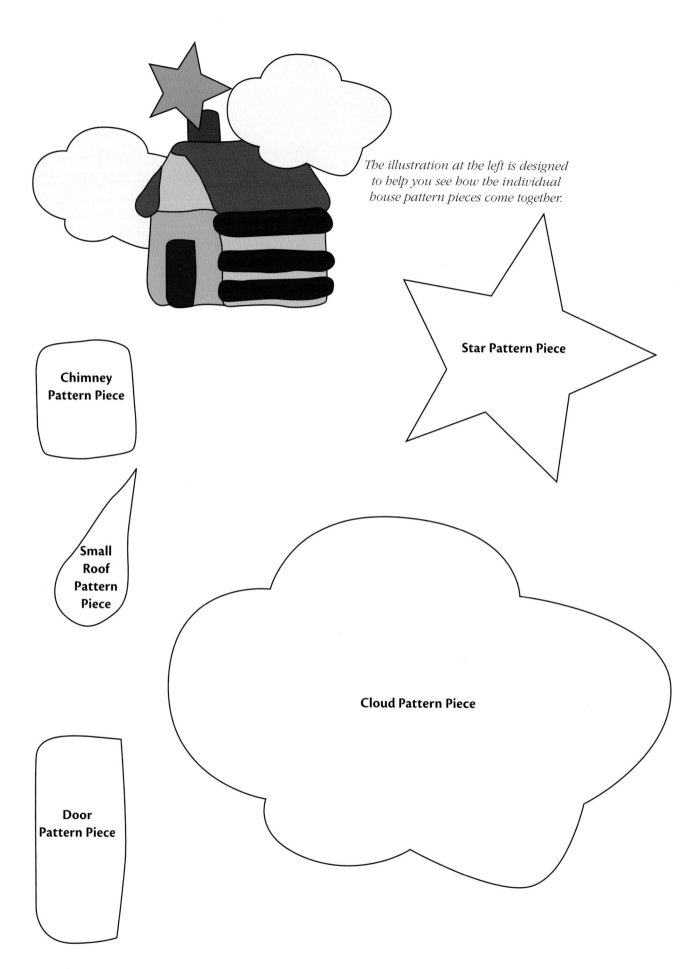

The illustration at the left is designed to help you see how the individual house pattern pieces come together.

Star Pattern Piece

Chimney Pattern Piece

Small Roof Pattern Piece

Cloud Pattern Piece

Door Pattern Piece

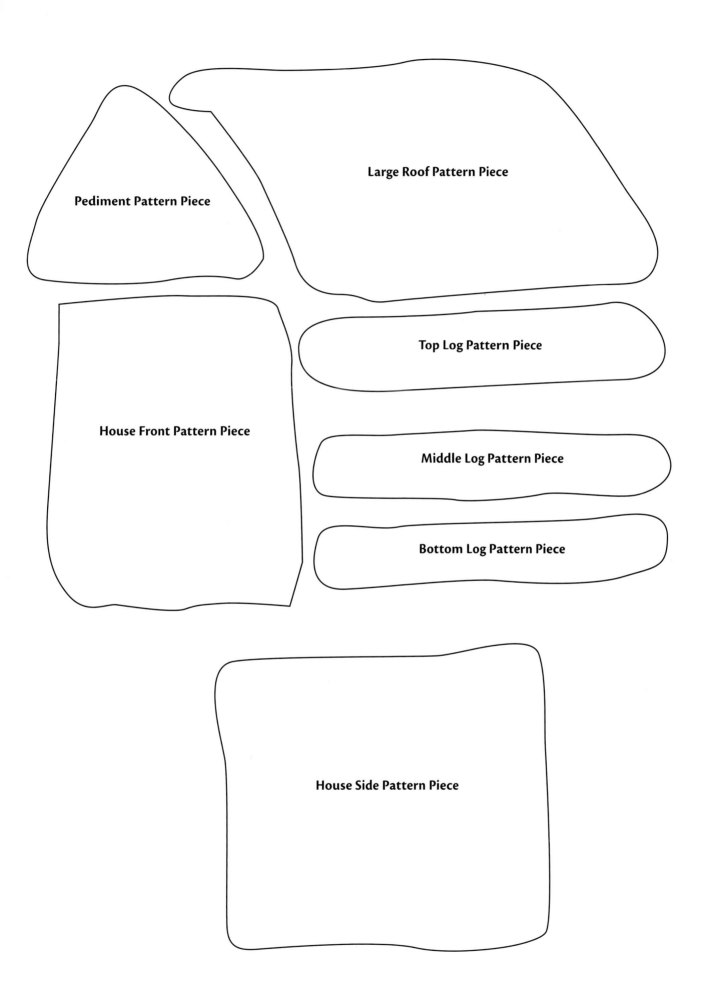

Pediment Pattern Piece

Large Roof Pattern Piece

House Front Pattern Piece

Top Log Pattern Piece

Middle Log Pattern Piece

Bottom Log Pattern Piece

House Side Pattern Piece

Autumn Trellis

When the blazing colors of summer fade, tranquil shades of rust and
brown are left. The uniqueness of this project is in the large number of
muted prints. Choose fabrics that are close in value and in tone.

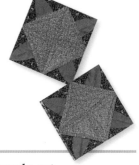

Materials Needed

- ¼-yard blue mini print
  (diamond flower centers)
- ¼-yard tan speckle
  (diamond flower centers)
- ¼-yard brown speckle
  (diamond flower centers)
- ¼-yard tan-and-purple fruit print
  (diamond flower centers)
- ¼-yard sage green (leaves)
- 1 yard rust-and-white print
  (flower backgrounds and border corners)
- ½-yard dark red print
  (flower backgrounds)
- ¼-yard burgundy (sashing)
- ¼-yard rust vine print (sashing)
- ¼-yard brown feather print (sashing)
- ¼-yard mauve toile (sashing)
- ⅛-yard mauve leaf print (sashing)
- ⅛-yard green stripe (sashing)
- ¼ yard green variegated (border)
- ½-yard dark brown leaf print (border)
- 44" square cotton fabric (backing)
- 44" square cotton quilt batting
- 5 yards 2½"-wide bias binding or
  prepackaged double-fold bias binding
- Coordinating thread
- 2 sheets 8½" x 11" tracing paper
- 2 sheets 8½" x 11" cardstock
- Air-soluble marking pen

Finished size: 43" square
The quilt measures 43½" square before quilting.
  The project will shrink slightly depending upon
  the amount of quilting.
Seam allowances: ¼"
Templates: Use the templates on page 119. Cut on
  the solid line and stitch on the broken line.

Cutting Plan

From the blue mini print, cut:
- 20 "A" triangles

From the tan speckle, cut:
- 16 "A" triangles

From the brown speckle, cut:
- 16 "A" triangles

**From the tan-and-purple
fruit print, cut:**
- 12 "A" triangles

From the sage green, cut:
- 32 "B" leaves

From the rust-and-white print, cut:
- 48 "C" shapes
- four "D" triangles

From the dark red print, cut:
- 16 "C" shapes

From the burgundy, cut:
- 25 3" squares

From the rust vine print, cut:
- 10 3" x 6¼" rectangles

From the brown feather print, cut:
- 12 3" x 6¼" rectangles

From the mauve toile, cut:
- eight 3" x 6¼" rectangles

From the mauve leaf print, cut:
- six 3" x 6¼" rectangles

From the green stripe, cut:
- four 3" x 6¼" rectangles

From the green variegated, cut:
- four 2" x 40" strips

From the dark brown leaf print, cut:
- four 2¾" x 40" strips

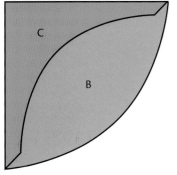

Diagram A-1

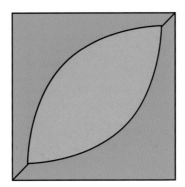

Diagram A-2

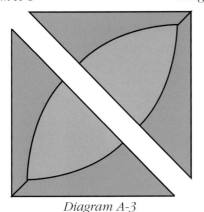

Diagram A-3

Make the Quilt Blocks

1 Match the curved shapes at the dots and stitch one rust-and-white "C" shape to the top of one "B" leaf, as shown in Diagram A-1. Review the instructions for Curved Patch Piecing on page 9 for assistance, if necessary. Press.

2 Stitch a matching rust-and-white "C" shape to the bottom of the same "B" leaf, as in Diagram A-2, to make a square. Press.

3 Repeat steps 1 and 2 to make a total of 24 rust leaf squares.

4 Repeat steps 1 and 2 again, but this time substitute dark red print "C" shapes for the rust-and-white "C" shapes to make a total of eight red leaf squares.

5 Cut both the rust leaf squares and the red leaf squares diagonally, as in Diagram A-3, to make 64 pieced triangles.

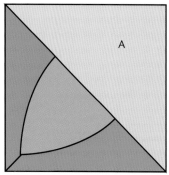

Diagram B-1

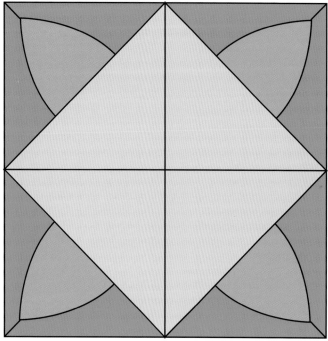

Diagram B-2

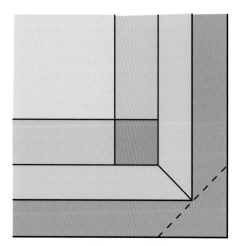

Diagram C-1

6 Stitch the long sides of four blue mini-print "A" triangles to the long sides of four rust pieced triangles, as in Diagram B-1, to create a square. Press.

7 Repeat step 6 with all 20 rust-blue pieced squares.

8 Stitch four rust-blue pieced squares together, as in Diagram B-2, to form a diamond in the center. Press.

9 Repeat step 8 to make a total of five blue diamond blocks.

10 Repeat steps 6 and 8, but this time substitute tan speckle "A" triangles for the blue mini-print to make four tan diamond blocks.

11 Repeat steps 6 and 8, but this time substitute tan-and-purple fruit print "A" triangles for the blue mini-print to make three fruit print diamond blocks.

12 Repeat steps 6 and 8, but this time substitute brown speckle "A" triangles for the blue mini-print and the red leaf pieces for the rust to make four brown diamond blocks.

Assemble the Quilt Top

1 Stitch together the quilt center using 3" burgundy squares, 3" x 6¼" rectangles and the various diamond blocks and following the Quilt Layout and its color code on the next page for placement.

2 Stitch the 2" x 40" green variegated strips to all four sides of the quilt center, starting and stopping ¼" from each edge.

3 Review the instructions for Mitered Corners on page 10 and miter the corners. Press.

4 Stitch the 2¾" x 40" dark brown print strips to all four sides of the quilt center. Press.

5 On the wrong side of the quilt, use the marking pen to mark diagonal lines at the corners, as shown on Diagram C-1.

6 Trim excess fabric to within ¼" of the marked lines.

7 Match the long sides of the rust-and-white print "D" triangles to the marked lines and stitch together to make the corners of the quilt top. Press.

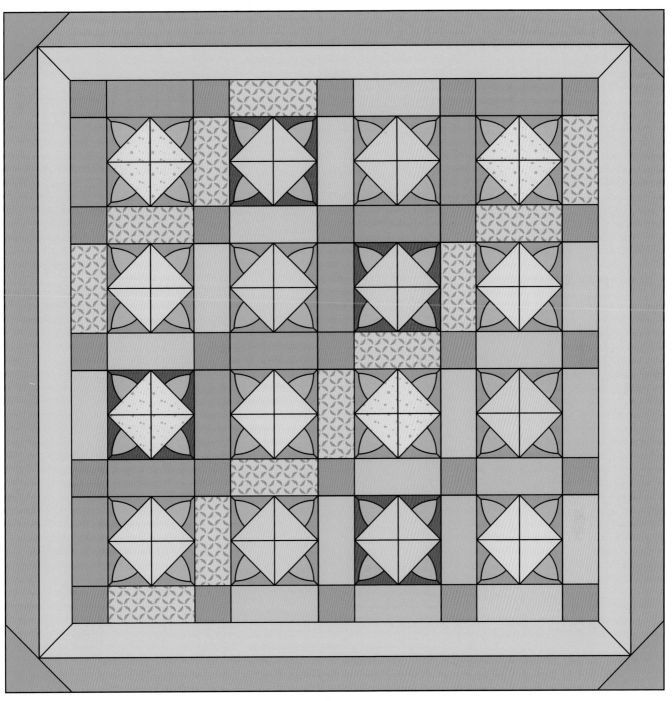

Quilt Layout

Sage Green	Tan Speckle	Mauve Toile
Green Variegated	Blue Mini Print	Mauve Leaf Print
Rust/White Print	Tan/Purple Fruit Print	Brown Feather Print
Burgundy	Brown Speckle	Green Stripe
Dark Red Print	Brown Leaf Print	Rust Vine Print

Finish the Quilt

The back of the quilt shows the detail of the machine quilting used for this particular design.

1 Review the instructions for Marking the Quilt Top on page 11 and mark the quilting lines on the quilt top with the marking pen.

2 With the wrong side up, place the backing fabric on the work surface. Carefully smooth out any folds and center the batting on the top of the backing fabric.

3 With the right side up, center the quilt top on the batting.

4 Baste through all layers with pins or with long basting stitches, referring back to the Pinning and Basting section on page 11 for assistance, if necessary.

5 Review the Machine Quilting instructions on page 11 and machine quilt as desired.

6 Remove pins or basting stitches.

7 Trim the thread ends and then trim the edge of the quilt.

8 Stitch the bias binding around the edge of the quilt, as detailed in the Binding instructions on page 11.

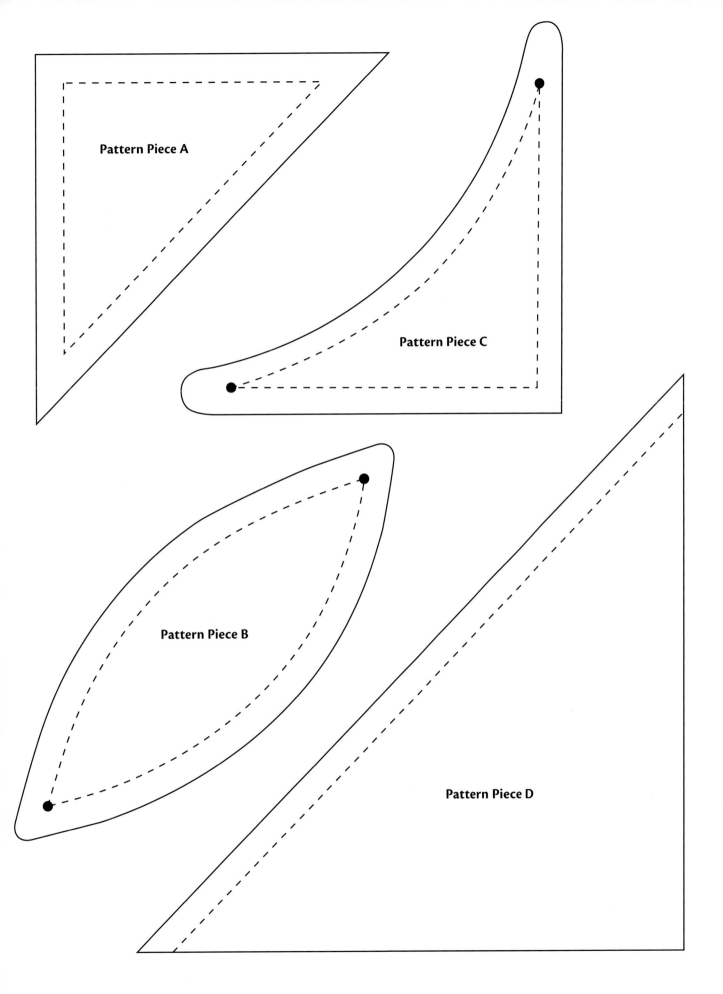

Pattern Piece A

Pattern Piece C

Pattern Piece B

Pattern Piece D

Snow Drift

A range of values, from sparkling white-on-white
to cool teal, create highlights and shadows in a
slice-of-time quilt of falling snowflakes.

Materials Needed

- 2 yards white-on-white print (snowflakes, ripple squares and border)
- ¾-yard blue speckle (snowflake background)
- ½-yard lavender (ripple squares)
- ½-yard lavender print (ripple squares)
- ½-yard light blue print (ripple squares)
- ½-yard blue (ripple squares)
- ¾-yard teal (ripple squares and snowflake corners)
- ¼-yard blue swirl print (bands)
- 46" x 56" rectangle cotton fabric (backing)
- 46" x 56" rectangle cotton quilt batting
- 5½ yards 2½"-wide bias binding or prepackaged double-fold bias binding
- Coordinating thread
- 1 sheet 8½" x 11" tracing paper
- 1 sheet 8½" x 11" cardstock
- Air-soluble marking pen

Finished size: 44½" x 55"

The quilt top measures 45" x 55½" before quilting. The project will shrink slightly depending on the amount of quilting.

Seam allowances: ¼"

Templates: Use the templates on page 125. Cut on the solid line and stitch on the broken line.

Cutting Plan

From the white-on-white print, cut:
- four 4¾" x 45" strips (Cut these long strips first.)
- 84 1¼" x 5" strips
- 14 "A" shapes
- 14 "B" shapes
- 14 3½" squares

From the blue speckle, cut:
- 84 "C" triangles

From the lavender, cut:
- 14 "A" shapes
- 14 "B" shapes

From the lavender print, cut:
- 28 3½" squares

From the light blue print, cut:
- 14 "A" shapes
- 14 "B" shapes

From the blue, cut:
- 14 "A" shapes
- 14 "B" shapes

From the teal, cut:
- 56 "D" shapes
- 14 3½" squares

From the blue swirl, cut:
- two 2¾" x 36½" strips

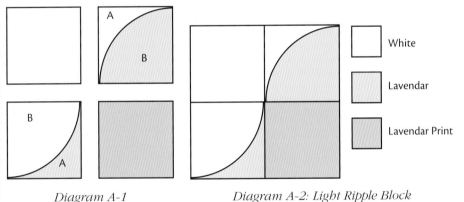

Diagram A-1

Diagram A-2: Light Ripple Block

White

Lavendar

Lavendar Print

Diagram B-1

Diagram B-2: Dark Ripple Block

Lavendar Print

Light Blue Print

Blue

Teal

Make the Quilt Blocks

1 Match the curved shapes at the dots and stitch specified "A" shapes to "B" shapes, as shown in Diagram A-1. Review the instructions for Curved Patch Piecing on page 9 for assistance, if necessary. Press.

2 Stitch the pieced "AB" squares together, as in Diagram A-2, to make a 6½" square. Press.

3 Repeat steps 1 and 2 to make a total of 14 light ripple blocks.

4 Repeat step 1, but this time using the "A" and "B" pieces in the colors specified in Diagram B-1.

5 Repeat step 2, using the "AB" blocks from step 4, to make a square like that in Diagram B-2.

6 Repeat steps 4 and 5 to make a total of 14 dark ripple blocks.

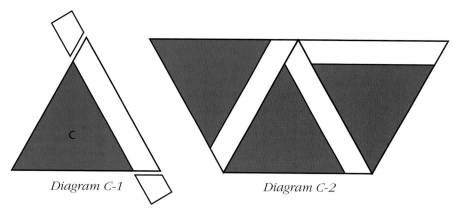

Diagram C-1   *Diagram C-2*

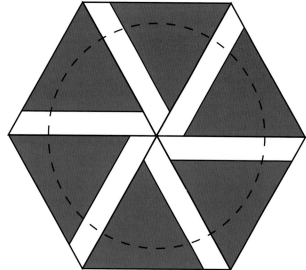

Diagram C-3

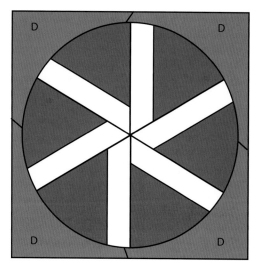

Diagram C-4: Snowflake Block

7 Center and stitch one 1¼" x 5" white strip to one side of a blue speckle "C" triangle and trim to make large triangle, as shown in Diagram C-1. Press.

8 Repeat step 7 for the remaining 83 triangles and strips for a total of 84 large white-blue triangles.

9 Stitch the long sides of six triangles together, beginning with three as in Diagram C-2, and adding in the other three to make a complete snowflake, as shown in Diagram C-3. Press.

10 Repeat step 9 to make a total of 14 snowflakes.

11 On the right side of the pieced snowflakes, center and mark a 6"-wide circle, as shown in Diagram C-3.

12 Place one snowflake on the work surface with a center seam vertical and stitch four "D" shapes at the corners to make a square, as shown in Diagram C-4. Press.

13 Repeat steps 11 and 12 with the remaining 13 snowflakes.

Assemble the Quilt Top

1 Stitch together the quilt center using the light ripple blocks, the dark ripple blocks and the snowflake blocks, as shown in the Quilt Layout on the next page. Press.

2 Stitch the 2¾" x 36½" blue swirl strips to the top and bottom of the quilt center. Press.

3 Stitch two 4¾" x 45" white strips to the sides of the quilt center. Press.

4 Stitch the remaining 4¾" x 45" white strips to the top and bottom of the quilt center. Press.

Quilt Layout

Finish the Quilt

1 Review the instructions for Marking the Quilt Top on page 11 and mark the quilting lines on the quilt top with the marking pen.

2 With the wrong side up, place the backing fabric on the work surface. Carefully smooth out any folds and center the batting on the top of the backing fabric.

3 With the right side up, center the quilt top on the batting.

4 Baste through all layers with pins or with long basting stitches, referring back to the Pinning and Basting section on page 11 for assistance, if necessary.

5 Review the Machine Quilting instructions on page 11 and machine quilt as desired.

6 Remove pins or basting stitches.

7 Trim the thread ends and then trim the edge of the quilt.

8 Stitch the bias binding around the edge of the quilt, as detailed in the Binding instructions on page 11.

9 Handstitch the buttons to the centers of the flowers.

The back of the quilt shows the detail of the machine quilting used for this particular design.

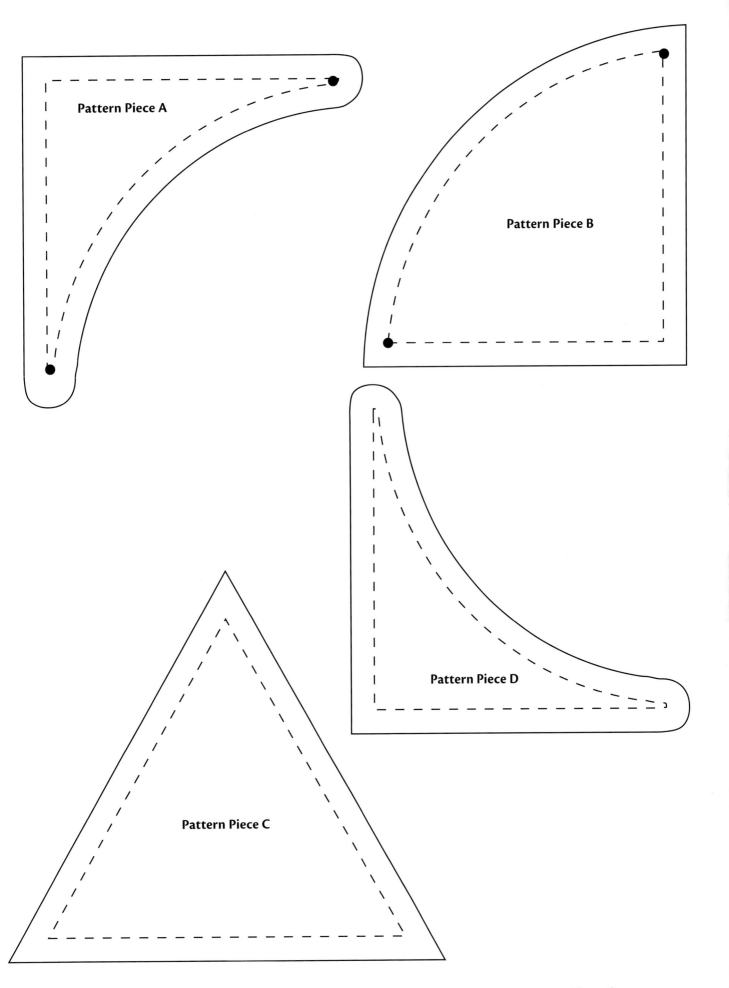

Pattern Piece A

Pattern Piece B

Pattern Piece D

Pattern Piece C

Resources

Benartex
(212) 840-3250
www.benartex.com
Fabric.

Coats & Clark
(800) 648-1479
www.coatsandclark.com
Thread.

DMC
(888) 610-1250
www.dmc-usa.com
Embroidery floss.

Fiskars Brands Inc.
(800) 500-4849
www.fiskars.com
Scissors.

Glorious Fabrics
(413) 367-2692
www.gloriousfabric.com
Fabric.

Hancock Fabrics
(877) 322-7427
www.hancockfabrics.com
Fabric.

Jinny Beyer
(866) 759-7373
www.jinnybeyer.com
Fabric.

JoAnn Fabrics
(888) 739-4120
www.joann.com
Fabric.

Kunin Felt
(603) 929-6100
www.kuninfelt.com
Felt.

Pellon
(919) 620-7457
www.pellonideas.com
Stabilizer.

Prym Dritz
(800) 255-7796
www.dritz.com
Sewing notions, air-soluble marking
pen.

River City Quilts
(507) 625-8136
www.rivercityquilts.com
Fabric.

Wrights
(800) 660-0415
www.wrights.com
Double-fold bias binding.

About the Author

Trice Boerens has authored many quilting, needlework and scrapbook books, and has designed fabrics, paper, stickers and jewelry. With a degree in art education from Brigham Young University, she is currently involved in teaching teen-agers in church and civic groups to design and assemble their own quilts. Awarded a National Printing Association Award of Excellence and the Anchor® Golden Needle Award, she also spends time researching quilting patterns and techniques from the 19th and early 20th centuries. Trice lives in the foothills of Utah's Wasatch Mountains with her husband and four children.

Also by Trice Boerens and available from KP Books: *Felt Art Accents for the Home* and *Sew and Quilt Japanese Décor.*

Create Beautiful PROJECTS WITH EASE

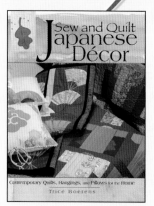